BIG
Dreams,
SMALL
Garden

BIG Dreams, SMALL Garden

A Guide to Creating Something Extraordinary in Your Ordinary Space

MARIANNE WILLBURN

Skyhorse Publishing

Skyhorse Publishing books may be purchased in bulk at special discounts for sales promotion, corporate gifts, fund-raising, or educational purposes. Special editions can also be created to specifications. For details, contact the Special Sales Department, Skyhorse Publishing, 307 West 36th Street, 11th Floor, New York, NY 10018 or info@skyhorsepublishing.com.

Skyhorse® and Skyhorse Publishing® are registered trademarks of Skyhorse Publishing, Inc.®, a Delaware corporation.

Visit our website at www.skyhorsepublishing.com.

10 9 8 7 6 5 4 3 2

Library of Congress Cataloging-in-Publication Data is available on file.

Cover design by Jane Sheppard
Cover photos: Marianne Willburn

Print ISBN: 978-1-5107-0912-6
Ebook ISBN: 978-1-5107-0913-3

Printed in China

To my father
Who has cultivated a spirit of profound
contentment and gratitude for as long as I can remember.

And my mother
Who taught me how to grow a bean, harvest a bean, cook a
bean, and can a bean—and still doesn't think she
knows what she's doing out there.

CONTENTS

Prologue   ix

Introduction   xi

SECTION ONE: VISUALIZE   1

Chapter 1   Why Create Eden?   3

Chapter 2   Recognizing and Accepting Limitations   17

Chapter 3   Accessing Your Creativity   31

Chapter 4   Planning Your Garden   43

SECTION TWO: ACHIEVE   59

Chapter 5   Tackling Garden Design   61

Chapter 6   Recognizing Resources   79

Chapter 7   Managing Your Garden Projects   93

Chapter 8   Building Skills   105

SECTION THREE: MAINTAIN   121

Chapter 9   Striking a Balance   123

Chapter 10   Making It Easier   135

Chapter 11   Enlisting the Troops   147

SECTION FOUR: ENJOY   161

Chapter 12   Living in the Eden You Have Created   163

Chapter 13   Reaching Out and Getting Better   173

Chapter 14   Cultivating a Spirit of Contentment   183

Epilogue   195

Works Cited   196

Recommended Books   197

Acknowledgments   198

Worksheets   200

PROLOGUE

O nce upon a time, there lived a gardener. She did not have the largest of gardens, nor the rarest, yet her garden gave her joy and inspired many to become gardeners themselves. One day, proud of her little oasis wedged tightly between the yards of her suburban neighbors, she decided to attend a high-profile garden tour and glean a few ideas off the creativity and budgets of other gardeners.

The sheer lavishness of the first two gardens surprised and delighted her, but by the third, green envy had begun to prick at her heart. By the fourth, she found herself staring not at the incredible rock garden, but at the finely manicured nails of her hostess as the woman painstakingly explained that the tufa boulders had been sourced and transported from Michigan quarries thousands of miles away.

The hands connected to those fingernails showed no sign of tufa damage, and our gardener hid her own chapped hands behind her back when her hostess complained of having very little help in the garden—only two staff gardeners three days a week.

Perhaps our gardener was a little sensitive that day on account of the car needing work and her daughter needing braces, but she found herself losing concentration. She passed through a knee-high forest of white and violet allium underplanted with forget-me-nots . . . and promptly forgot them. The raking sunlight had turned the magnolia blossoms translucent, which in turn lit up the field poppies at their feet, but she had stopped paying attention by then.

Instead, mental calculations had begun, and she unhappily heard herself asking another visitor the dangerous, age-old question that helps us all determine our pecking order in this world, "What does she do for a living?"

She didn't like the answer, which neatly played into all the stereotypes regarding wealth she had ever held, but after a restorative glass of pinot grigio in a nearby café before the next tour, she decided she had a choice to make.

If she was foolish, she could spend the rest of the day comparing her tiny resources to those of her hostess—ending with an envious wine-fueled rant at dinnertime upon the inequities of this world and the reasons why Marie Antoinette didn't see her thirty-eighth birthday.

But if she was smart, she'd pull out her camera, pull out her notebook, and start paying attention.

And then she'd go home and write a book.

INTRODUCTION

Creating the garden that lives somewhere deep inside you is difficult when you honestly assess your living situation and it bears no resemblance to the well-structured fantasy you constructed at the tender age of twenty.

Over a decade ago, in October of 2008, the world changed drastically. And it changed so drastically that even gardeners, with our hearts firmly in the soil but our financial heartbeats tied to mortgages, loans, retirement accounts, and investment strategies, had to dust off our hands and pay attention—joining millions of others in the feeling that we were not actually in control of our financial destiny.

Good decisions we might have made, such as fully funding those retirement accounts, or taking out a smaller mortgage than we could afford, suddenly became bad decisions as the job and stock markets plummeted and options became scarce. Now we had very little to show for years of saving. Now we couldn't afford to move out of the starter home we had thought was such a good investment just a few years before.

Now we had to adjust our dreams. Some of us just plain lost them.

My husband and I both grew up in the country, and as children we enjoyed the pleasures of rural living and the luxury of space. My parents were avid gardeners, who, in turn, imparted that love to their children.

However, young adults can't be told how good they've got it. In pursuit of education, jobs, and the age-old draw of big city excitement, we moved to large cities with tiny homes and tinier gardens only to spend the next twenty years trying to beat a path back to sanity.

My first garden was a two-by-seventeen-foot strip in a parking lot that provided tomatoes but elicited chuckles from my Southern California twenty-something friends. My second garden consisted of two large window boxes and an arrangement of wildly sophisticated, yet continuously stolen, pots in a dodgy South London neighborhood. When we moved back to America and I started to landscape every inch of our tiny rental garden in a small suburban neighborhood, my husband announced it was time to grow up and buy a house.

My first strip garden. Most of my twentysomething friends were too busy stripping to notice.

We did, and we bought well within our means, ignoring the pleas of our realtor to buy something that matched our income or even pushed it a little bit. Sure we wanted the eighteenth-century Federal home with bank barn and ten acres—just like anyone else who had dreams and subscriptions to posh gardening magazines—but we felt that if we moved carefully and frugally we might have a better chance of attaining that dream in the future.

The house was small, drafty, and run-down, but the gorgeous country acre was a paradise to hands that ached to create something of their own. Sadly, those hands had about eighteen months to plant a dogwood, sketch some plans, and play in the dirt between diaper changes before paradise was lost in a surprise corporate layoff. One step forward, two steps back.

We sold the house, circled the wagons, and put our massive student loans into forbearance, rapidly erasing all the headway we'd made on principal in the previous two years. After a year of tirelessly job hunting, a brief stint on food stamps, and serious plans to go home and live with my parents with two kids in tow, my husband took a significant pay cut to secure a

Big Dreams, Small Garden

A little ambitious, but I dreamed of such things.

job in another county. In time, we managed to purchase another small fixer-upper in a little town on a commuter train line.

I clearly remember looking at the *tiny* sloped garden that wasn't a garden, thinking of my lost acre, and asking aloud, "What on earth can I do with this?" My husband looked at the garden that wasn't a garden and said, "Don't worry about it, we'll only be here for three years."

Had he multiplied that number by four, he would have been closer.

We stayed. We renovated. We took years off our lives through plaster dust inhalation and chemical paint stripper fumes. Meanwhile, the cost of homes with land was going through the roof, and the modest gains we might have made on our home if we sold it couldn't possibly offset one of those mortgages.

However, as much we wanted to listen to the sweet words of crooked loan officers and mortgage bankers, we *knew* we couldn't afford what they were selling. We played it safe and stayed put.

Gray, uninspiring, and run-down. And that was just the land.

Others weren't so careful. The overinflated market collapsed, negating years of sweat equity and weekends at home improvement stores, and, once again, we were at the mercy of other people's bad decisions.

Now, the dream of owning and gardening more land than a tenth of an acre in the middle of a busy town became a *very* far off reality. No matter that we'd stuck to a policy of no credit card debt or car loans or recreational shopping for as-seen-on-TV gadgets. Other people had, and still others had given them all the credit they needed in order to do so. Consequently, we were looking at a deflated retirement account, a deflated home value, and deflated dreams.

We met many others in the same leaking boat who were just as bewildered as we were. The property ladder was now a property chute. Who changed the rule book while we weren't looking?

During the first couple of years in our "new" old house I grappled with envy.

I grappled with anger and injustice and all of the yucky, sticky emotions whose very invocation makes you feel even worse about yourself. After all, we were healthy, we had two wonderful children, we were employed again, and, however drafty, we had a roof over our heads. But we didn't want to be HERE. We'd made good choices, educated ourselves, invested wisely, and always lived far below our means. Why hadn't all those things added up to the home and garden of our dreams, or at least a small hope that we could attain it before we no longer had the energy to create it?

At the time, a beloved aunt of mine told me that if you could write a check to solve a problem, it wasn't a terrible problem. They were wise words, and I knew them to be true, but I still felt a deep sense of grief for the opportunities that had been lost through no fault of our own. Sure, a hypothetical check *could* be written, but there wasn't much chance of it actually *being* written in the near future by either one of us.

There were others writing checks, of course. That same aunt ran a prestigious travel booking service for the extremely rich in a very desirable area of California. Her clients booked rooms at eleven hundred dollars a night. They paid one thousand dollars for lunch for two at world-renowned restaurants, and had massage therapists follow them throughout their weekend away. Her business hardly felt the ping of 2008.

Channeling energy into my garden had a remarkable healing effect upon my state of mind.

Although I knew that people were much worse off than we were, envy still peppered my thoughts, and though I was outwardly smiling and trying to be grateful for what we had, I couldn't help thinking how removed many people were from the real-life heartbreaks stemming from the financial crises—both the dotcom bust of the early millennium that had thrown our family into reverse gear, and the new banking implosion that hit everyone in the pocket and provided the one-two punch to our home and garden dreams. It's hard to get over envy and anger like that, particularly when one feels justified.

In my darker moments, I had half a mind to go spend a few nights in solidarity with the Occupy movement in a public park, but I realized we'd only end up arguing over private property rights and what kind of music to play over the campfire at night. Instead, I bought a T-shirt from a favorite plant nursery that read, "Occupy. The Garden."

My saving grace *became* my garden. There, in a marginal lot surrounding a rundown house, in a neighborhood that didn't "do" gardens, in a town struggling with broken promises of revitalization and renewal, I picked up my trowel and started again.

I was fortunate. The quiet voice inside me never told me to stop gardening, to wait for the right house, the right income, or the right time. It just told me that I needed the garden.

Other voices weren't so quiet.

"Why spend your energy?" I heard many times, especially from well-meaning friends who lived on farms or acreage, or from out-of-town visitors who would survey the lack of care evident in neighboring homes and wonder why we were making our home the best on the block.

"Why not flip it and get a better house?" asked suburbanite friends, whose goals for more home square footage and a theater room bore no resemblance to our goals for square acreage and a chicken coop.

Neighbors watched with incredulity as we painted the house, designed and built our own deck on the cheap, hauled two thousand free bricks out of the town landfill, and filled the space with free plants, honey-producing bees, and at one point, yes, even "illegal" chickens.

At the end of ten productive and beautifying years, and four years after the market crash, we still couldn't afford to buy a house with land, but it was generally agreed that we had one of the loveliest homes and gardens in town: a garden that capitalized on a high hilltop view, screened out everything else, and generally acted as a serene retreat at the end of a long, busy day.

Things weren't perfect. I couldn't have backyard chickens and couldn't persuade the town to change its ridiculous ordinance. We dealt with the annoyance of an antiquated town emergency siren that would go off unexpectedly, signaling a Blitzkrieg air attack seventy years too late. Relations with certain neighbors were often strained, resulting from the "new vs. old" mentality that

Ten years later, a bit of paint and a mature garden made this house feel like home.

infected the town and labeled us squarely as newcomers. We still wanted to move, still wanted land, still hoped that skimming the real estate sections each Saturday morning would discover us a prize property at an affordable price before anybody else could get there first.

But when it didn't appear, there were always Saturday nights in the Eden we'd created. Friends wanted to come over and sit on the deck or wander through the scent-filled borders at twilight with a glass of wine in hand.

There were vegetables to pick—sometimes in unexpected places—and bees to watch from the comfort of an old swing. Rambling roses grew up the south side of the house, climbing hydrangeas on the north, and hardy kiwis and hop vines staked their claim on the west-facing deck. Life was good in this six thousand-square-foot oasis.

Then something unexpected and wonderful happened, as these things will when you let go of unhelpful emotions, or at the very least, laugh at them. I started to write again. This time about my garden and the many ways in which it enriched us, particularly in reminding us that life wasn't about what you don't have, but about what you do with what you have. I met many people through my writing, subsequent lectures, and walks through the garden; I met many more through clubs I was invited to join or to whom I was asked to speak.

All because of a garden I never intended to call mine.

∽

Perhaps you're in a similar situation: living many years in a house and garden that you only expected to occupy for a little while until you found your dream property. Perhaps your neighborhood changed radically, and when the huge lovely lots that flanked your house became fodder for contract-hungry developers, there were twenty new windows peering onto your private patio.

Maybe you're trapped in an HOA that makes you want to tear your hair out, or at least the hair of the neighbor who consistently calls the management company every time you add an unsanctioned gazing ball to the front garden.

You might be renting a home longer than you thought, or renting an apartment when you thought you'd be in a home. You might want chickens in your backyard and don't live in an enlightened urban area, or perhaps you want bees and your next door neighbor just informed you she almost died in 1984 from playing barefoot in the clover.

And then, of course, there are the stories of loss.

Stories of achieving your dream garden, putting your heart and soul into it, and then suffering a job loss or other major change of circumstance that forces you to move to something smaller, something that you no longer love.

Whatever your situation, you feel your blood boil when a well-meaning friend asks "When are you going to move?" or a less

We lost our first home, but kept a little of the garden with us. This yellow iris has been planted at the entrance of every home since.

well-meaning city code enforcement officer tells you "If you don't like it, move." Moving is not an option—at least not now, nor for a good while longer. You are part of the 99 percent, and money is definitely an object.

The trouble is, you're also a gardener, and you've got dreams.

This book is about finding those dreams, wherever you are and with whatever you have. It is about *finding contentment wherever you find yourself.*

It will help you see the extraordinary in your ordinary, mapping the process every step of the way from the difficulties of visualization to the blessings of enjoyment. It is about the *joy of gardening*—a joy that, thankfully, can be found on a micro level. And that's a good thing, because if you're anything like the vast majority of the other ninety-niners out there, you've got micro in abundance.

Any overwhelming task must be split into sections, and creating a garden with little in the way of resources and much in the way of obstacles is no exception. The book is therefore divided into four parts: Visualize, Achieve, Maintain, and Enjoy. The chapters within those sections guide you to look beyond Madison Avenue marketing teams and give yourself the permission to put together an amazing garden on your own terms.

During this process, don't be surprised if you find that twenty-year-old dreamer within you once again. Releasing our envy, our anger, and our sense of injustice is a natural result of allowing the garden to connect us to our true place on this earth and alert us to the daily miracles that surround us no matter how much money we have. It gives us an opportunity for healing, for connection, and for peace. Only then can we truly benefit from new opportunities in our lives, moving forward with joy and contentment instead of anxiety and resentment.

I invite you to join me as we travel this path together; embracing the space around us, *right here, right now*, and gardening the hell out of it. A garden doesn't have to be perfect. In the middle of August, it doesn't even have to be green. It just has to be yours. That's enough. I promise.

SECTION ONE
VISUALIZE

1

WHY CREATE EDEN?

"In the depths of winter, I finally learned that within me there lay an invincible summer."
—Albert Camus

"When are you guys going to get yourselves some property, anyway?"

The words came from a friend of mine, safely settled for ten years on her six-acre farm with bank barn, eighteenth-century stone house, and boxwood-lined herb garden just off the kitchen door. But on that May afternoon, we were sitting on my porch, sharing a beer, and surveying the small town garden around us from the comfort of well-loved wicker chairs.

The garden was outdoing itself that day. Scents, textures, and colors mingled heavily together and intoxicated the senses without any help from the beer. Larkspur shot purple rockets into the sky. Alchemilla spilled onto the gravel paths. Ajuga popped from between brick pavers, and the privet was frosted with tiny white flowers that hummed with bees. Each element gave every indication of being part of an ideal country garden . . . Eden on earth.

Yet, had we risen from our seats, walked under the wisteria arbor, and unlatched the gate leading out onto the street, we would have been greeted by a very different scene: parked cars, rusting bikes, faded houses, and one or two barking dogs sharing space with dilapidated lawn furniture; the very scene my eyes took in the day we moved into the house ten years before.

Except on that day, I was standing on my own dilapidated porch surrounded by grass and cement, and there was no gate to unlatch.

My friend's words were meant in all kindness, the result of an afternoon's discussion of seed starting and canning techniques to process the glut of produce coming out of the vegetable garden in the back. In her mind, it didn't make sense that a couple like my husband and I, committed to an outdoor life, the home economy, and the pleasures of the garden should still be living in a small home on a tiny lot in the middle of town after ten years.

I smiled lazily and replied, "I need an undergardener before I take on even a tenth of an acre more," and refilled her glass from the bottle sitting between us. But as I sat back and continued to drink in the sights and smells of the surrounding garden, I couldn't help but remember how differently that question had affected me ten or so years previously.

And it was a question I heard all the time.

One would think that the forced, thin smile that such a query elicited from me in those days would have been enough to stop even the least tactful of friends and acquaintances. After all, most of them knew of the financial upheaval that a year's layoff had created in our lives. Quite frankly, we were lucky to have a roof over our heads, dilapidated porch or no. Our "new" old house needed much in the way of money and much in the way of time, and I was homeschooling my five-year-old with a toddler who had a fast pair of legs and a fascination for ancient electrical plugs. We'd lost our acre in the country, our lack of neighbors, our rural dreams, and our sense of adventure had been smothered in the bargain.

I stared at that porch, and I stared at that neighborhood, and I did not feel grateful. I felt angry. A tight smile was about all I could manage in the face of what I perceived to be such injustice.

Privacy lost. By the end of ten years, another two houses had been added along this line.

Big Dreams, Small Garden

Yet, here I was, ten years later, sitting on that same porch, infused with a spirit of contentment. Still with dreams in tow—still excited by the next phase of life and the next open door. But softly and curiously content.

I might have created the garden, but it was the garden that created that sense of peace in me.

Privacy regained. The upper terrace softly blocked neighboring windows with forsythia, euonymus, privet, and various perennials, while the bottom terrace housed a playhouse made from used materials and a vegetable garden.

I didn't need any convincing to start working on a garden where there wasn't one, but I'm a gardener *at heart*, and the fact that you're reading these words probably means you're one too, even if you're struggling with overwhelming feelings of "Why bother?" and "How will I ever?" at the moment.

Gardeners are a strange group of people. Even without a garden to tend, we're nuts, we're enthusiastic, and we're very serious. If you're one of us, you know it, and chances are you've known it for a very long time.

Consider:

- What is it that makes a twentysomething plant a median strip with tomato plants instead of hanging out with friends after work?
- What is it that makes a thirtysomething plan family holidays to coincide with open days at great gardens?
- What is it that makes a forty- or a fiftysomething pay good money to hike with a stranger in a foreign country searching for wildflowers when they should be flirting with a stranger in a foreign country and searching for sangria?

My husband has told me that the answer to the first two questions is "insanity," and the answer to the third is "middle age," but you and I both know better on this one. It is the infectious joy of gardening.

Don LaFond, a superb rock gardener and plant breeder in Michigan, has possibly the best description of gradually succumbing to this infection. "One day I was wandering around a rock garden with my wife, looking at trees and wondering why so many crazy people were clustered around a microscopic plant for twenty minutes," he remembers fondly, "and three years later, *I* was one of those crazy people."

Gardeners have a fundamental advantage when life drills a hole in the boat and reality starts to go soggy. There are simply more reasons to get out there and garden than there are reasons not to, and each and every one of them promotes mental and physical well-being. It's precisely what you need when you are frantically bailing water and looking for the shore.

Let's look at a few of my favorites:

Connection

You know if you're one of us.

Regardless of how deep (and how crazy) your passion takes you, you fundamentally understand that gardening connects us to the part of our environment that isn't plastic, doesn't come in neat packaging, and provides simple purpose when our modern lives seem ever more urbanized and complicated. We wear synthetic clothes and drink chemical reactions every day, but in the garden we are greeted with real scents, real beauty, real textures, and the miraculous cycle of real life playing out before us over days, weeks, months, and years.

It feels good to get outside after a day spent in a cubicle or office or at home washing endless loads of laundry. It feels good to stretch your limbs and remember muscles you had a passing acquaintance with back in high school. It's a reconnection with our place in Earth's fragile, beautiful ecosystem—and a reminder that the deadlines, sports practices, parent/teacher meetings, and horrible bosses are just a superficial layer, not a state of being.

My father worked three jobs while attending graduate school and supporting a family in the early seventies. My mother's sandwiches packed at 4:30 every morning might have kept him alive, but to this day he credits their small vegetable garden and a push mower with

The reawakening of the earth each spring connects every living thing.

keeping him sane and healthy. "Getting out there, weeding, mowing, digging . . . I needed that," he said wistfully, thinking back on those difficult years.

A reconnection with nature is something we all crave, whether gardener or not. Some of us take it in the form of a holiday, others in the form of a television documentary. But those of us who choose to get out there and experience it for ourselves on a daily basis know there is something more to it, even if we can't quite find the words to describe what "it" really is.

Food freedom

It is highly doubtful that the first humans to plant seeds ten thousand years ago were planting zinnia or poppies to grace the tabletops for late-night dinner parties. Gardening, first and foremost, was about nourishment, and continues to be about nourishment for many to this day. There are two things at work here: one, the freedom to feed your family with fresh, healthy vegetables; and two, the freedom to feed your family with fresh, healthy vegetables *when money is tight.*

You can't eat fresher vegetables than those you grow yourself.

If you consider yourself a foodie, meaning you are not only concerned with *what* you eat and how it's prepared, but *where* it came from and how it got to your kitchen, then you're probably amazed by the mainstreaming of monikers such as "organic" and "heirloom" in recent years, and just how much money those two words can squeeze out of consumer wallets.

If you are what I like to call a "seasoned foodie," that is, a person who was paying attention to these same things twenty-plus years ago when it wasn't cool, then you're probably smirking at the circus going on right now and fuming that it's getting more expensive to attend.

Just because we don't have the budget to pay four dollars and ninety-nine cents for a pound of tomatoes and pick up a head of butter lettuce at four dollars a pop doesn't mean we don't deeply value the freshest and healthiest of ingredients. It just means Junior needs a new pair of shoes and the car needs tires.

This is where our gardens come in.

There is nothing quite so satisfying as eating something you grew through the work of your own hands, particularly when you know it's being sold down the road for ten times the price.

"Let them eat cake!" said the ill-fated Marie Antoinette to a starving 99 percent more than two hundred years ago. I have to confess to a guilty pleasure in telling the Antoinettes of this world, "Let them eat overpriced niche market vegetables!" I'm enjoying the same thing for much less *chez moi*.

Fitness

Gardening is exercise, pure and simple. Regular hard work outside will strengthen and tone muscles, burn fat, and, speaking as one who has hauled twenty-five hundred bricks

The author building her muscles during a community garden workday.

out of a landfill, can significantly increase endurance. However, as sweat and dirt are not the tidiest of bedfellows, and garden fashion is not as likely to get you noticed as a pair of yoga pants and a sports bra, gardening is not usually seen as the hippest way of keeping fit.

If you are turned off by the pairing of sweat and soil, I'm afraid I must ask you to please put down this book, get a gym membership for your fashionable fitness needs, and marry an heir or heiress to support your expensive habit. With limited funds, you don't have the option to hire someone to do most of the heavy work; but the good news is, your body is likely to reflect that socioeconomic reality every time you stand naked in front of the mirror.

Apart from a brisk walk every morning, gardening really is my choice of exercise. I have never been particularly excited about indoor/outdoor carpet and wiping someone else's sweat off a weight bench. Lifting, bending, hauling, stretching, pulling, pushing, and, yes, sometimes even therapeutic moaning, all contribute to a healthier me, and what could be better than feeling fit AND creating a beautiful space at the same time?

Separation

Do you ever have a disagreement with someone you live with and just need to be left alone in peace and quiet? What happens if that disagreement is with a difficult neighborhood . . . every day? While I don't condone Garboesque solitude, or intentionally drawing away from making relationships with neighbors that might ultimately enrich our lives, I also feel strongly that creating a private, special space outside can have a healing effect upon us, especially when we're feeling vulnerable.

At first, our neighbors were very suspicious when we built a fence around our little property and assumed it was an attempt to "remove" ourselves from the neighborhood. Though they were mistaken in this assumption, there were, however, very real physical concerns that we addressed by building that fence. For one, an aggressive dog on a long chain next door and my fearless toddler did not a match in heaven make. For another, having neighborhood kids ride their bikes over my front flower beds as a shortcut home was giving me the reputation of being a screaming banshee.

After losing our rural home with very few neighbors and a whole lot of outside elbow room, it was a shock to be rubbing those elbows with so many others. I didn't particularly want to witness a domestic argument going on a few doors down or hear a middle school child swear like a sailor. And I certainly didn't want to eat al fresco spaghetti bolognese on my porch at night only to watch my neighbor across the street eat hers. It became clear that boundaries were needed.

However, it was more than just dogs and badly behaved children. Building a fence gave me a boundary against which to plant and create a restful place with a beginning and an end. Ironically, creating this separation boundary gave us the ability to invite others *into* that space, to benefit from that sense of peace and tranquility, and allow them to separate from the hustle and bustle of their lives.

One of the very best compliments I ever heard about my garden came from a neighbor, and eventual dear friend, who brought her four-year-old daughter over to play with my children one day. As they approached the gate, I heard my friend say softly, "Wait." All was quiet for a moment, and then I heard her whisper, "One, two, three. Okay . . . open the door to Narnia."

That's worth building a garden for.

Pride of place

Gardening not only creates a sense of pride for the gardener, but for his or her neighborhood, apartment or condo complex, or development. It truly is a win–win situation. This pride can be infectious, inspiring others to take more time with their properties, and, as a result, create a more beautiful, unified community from the inside out.

For those of us who found ourselves somewhere we didn't expect to be as a result of something we didn't expect to happen, this reason for gardening our space may ring a little hollow. I can hear the indignant cries even as I type these words.

"Pride? In our place?!?"
"I don't belong here!"
"This isn't my choice!"
"This isn't my community!"

I can't tell you the amount of times I have walked through an average neighborhood or been in a dodgy end of town and been stopped in my tracks by the

Never underestimate the joy you can bring into the lives of others through your garden.

simple beauty of a grouping of well-planted pots or window boxes. Just for a second, the person who created that little tableau inserted joy into my day and reminded me that you never know when it's going to come along.

Leading by example is the best way of converting others, particularly when you share many of the same concerns and obstacles they have. And, as one more adventurous soul joins the merry band of brother gardeners, we all benefit as a community.

Acceptance and understanding

Envy is a destructive emotion. If you let it, it can somehow insert itself into every conversation and every thought—even your best ones. If you find yourself mentally adding the words "nice for some" to the end of a long story about someone else's vacation, new home, or good fortune, chances are you're struggling with this dark emotion and not winning.

Years ago, a coworker of mine was complaining about the torn curtains literally rotting in the front room of her rented flat. Having spent years sewing cheap treatments for windows to brighten up rented apartments, I exclaimed, "Replace them!"

"Why should I?" she said indignantly, "I don't own the flat."

"But you live there." I challenged her. "You've lived there for ten years. It's your home."

"Nevertheless," she stated, ending the discussion. She passed the wine and changed the subject.

Let's think about this for a minute shall we? Would you rather stare at ugly, rotting curtains every day and grow ever more resentful over the larger picture of where you are and where you may or may not be going, or replace them with something that makes you smile, even if it's as simple as a quilt from Goodwill held up with a few clothespins?

When you open your door and go outside, what "rotting curtains" do you see? There are problem areas in a garden, and then there are problem gardens, period. Poor drainage, terrible views, a neighbor with a security light fixation, barking dogs, chain-link fences, no fences, steep hills, deep gullies, dry shade, rocky soil, and a hundred other issues that can, and often do, stop us from enjoying the place where life has placed us for a year, five years, or two decades.

But we must claim our living spaces, whatever they are, because they are just that—our living spaces. We nest here. We raise our kids, live our heartbreaks, and experience some of our greatest joys here. For gardeners, would-be gardeners, and if-only-I-had-the-perfect-place gardeners, we cheat ourselves if we keep waiting.

The great news is, the very act of claiming that space through gardening can help us shelve that envy and build a better way of thinking, pot by pot, shovelful by shovelful, eventually leading us to a place where our dreams still exist, but where they are no longer tarnished by anger and resentment. Instead, our inner contentment allows us to access them once again. And, we end up with fresh tomatoes.

Are those enough reasons for you? Right. Let's get on with it then.

THE URBAN HOMESTEAD

O n a tenth of an acre plot in one of the busiest sections of Pasadena, California, the Dervaes family has been edibly landscaping every square inch of their space since the mid-eighties to an average tune of six thousand pounds of produce a year. Disaffected with the consumer culture at large, yet unable to afford the five acres of self-sufficiency they longed for, former school-teacher Jules Dervaes and his three children began tearing out front lawns, shocking the neighbors and making their urban space a beautiful working farm that has inspired countless people worldwide to innovate in the most unlikely of spaces.

Sadly, Jules passed away in December of 2016, but I was lucky enough to speak to him severa months before he died about creating this beautiful way of life for himself and three of his now growr children, Anais, Justin, and Jordanne. They continue to run the farm today with the many skills their father helped them to build.

Jules never accepted excuses in pursuing his dream. Neighboring freeway? They've got it. Poo soil? They had it. Difficult neighborhood? Their example and outreach over the last thirty years changed it. "If you wait, you might never have it; you could waste your life waiting," said Jules. He

knew what he was talking about. The Dervaes family plan was to live in their house for four years. Four years turned into three decades.

During those years the urban lot has been transformed into an edible paradise and a teaching platform, but not without a great deal of trial and error. "I went through what I like to call my 'brown phase,'" Jules told me with a chuckle. "There wasn't anyone to copy back then. We got here from a lot of mistakes." The small space forced the family to adapt and learn new skills, but it also kept them from biting off more than they could chew. Even after all this time however, the family still looks forward to someday doing the same thing with more land in a partnership with others who share a core value of leaving the planet better than they found it—many of those kindred spirits follow the famous farm at UrbanHomestead.org.

The interview with Jules was a memorable one, and sometimes when I'm feeling overwhelmed, I reflect upon the words he spoke at the end of our conversation. "I have to remind people that it took us thirty years to build all of this," he told me. "Even if you have the skills and know everything, it still takes time."

2

RECOGNIZING AND ACCEPTING LIMITATIONS

"To overcome difficulties is to experience the full delight of existence."
—Arthur Schopenhauer

L et's talk limitations. Our lives (and our gardens) are directed by the choices we must make based upon the limitations of our space, time, energy, and, of course, money. Though we are culturally programmed these days to see these choices as negative, limitations can be freeing in many ways.

It's very important to understand that there are as many different levels of hardship in this lovely world as there are people to populate it. The lady at the beginning of the book who complained about having gardening staff only three days a week (yes, that really happened), doesn't understand that I cannot share her perception of such luxury as a hardship. And although I cannot imagine having a gardener working for me, I also have a hard time remembering what it was like to consider a one dollar and twenty-cent bus fare a splurge when I was twenty-seven and living on a desperately tiny budget.

So, as we travel through this chapter and consider our limitations, put your prejudices and envies aside and look only at your situation right here, right now. Don't compare it with mine, with hers, or with that supercilious frenemy you keep running into at the dog park. We've all got obstacles, they're just different. Let's look at them with a desire to solve them, not rank them, or worse, wallow in them.

Letting go

A preconceived notion of what a garden should be is our absolute worst enemy in the quest to create our own. We build and reinforce these pictures in our brains over time and with

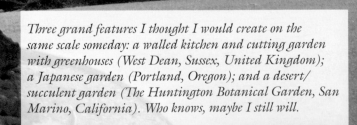

Three grand features I thought I would create on the same scale someday: a walled kitchen and cutting garden with greenhouses (West Dean, Sussex, United Kingdom); a Japanese garden (Portland, Oregon); and a desert/succulent garden (The Huntington Botanical Garden, San Marino, California). Who knows, maybe I still will.

the aid of magazines, books, and other sources of garden porn. As we will discuss later, these sources can be inspiring, but they can also set us up for discontent.

Fifty-foot-long perennial borders, wrought iron gates, a majestic meadow with rustic bluebird houses . . . if you are only able to imagine a water feature as a ten-by-twenty-foot pond with a waterfall and seventeen full-size koi, you will only be disappointed by anything else. Holding onto the idea of something you have always wanted but cannot have in the present only contributes to a sense of discontent and dissatisfaction.

So, how do we break the mindset? Here are four things to consider every time you find yourself grappling with garden envy.

Big garden = big price
Remind yourself that a large garden requires a large amount of time, thought, and financial outlay, whereas a small garden can give one a sense of joy and accomplishment whilst allowing greater balance in the rest of one's life. More is not always better.

Small garden = a chance to shine
Most people given forty acres and four million dollars can create a fabulous garden. Doing so on a marginal tenth of an acre with the leftover clothing and food budget takes the soul of a gardener—and it shows.

Make it a game
There are two ways to look at shopping at thrift stores for watering cans, picking up patio furniture on the side of the road, and digging more than two thousand bricks out of a dirt pile on a hot summer's day: because you *have* to, or because you *want* to. When you make frugality and clever use of resources a game, you short-circuit the envy and resentment feedback loop in your brain.

Mind how you go
We've all heard a lot about mindfulness these days, and it no longer means how to treat a fellow human being or board a subway train. Mindfulness is the practice of focusing your attention deliberately on the present moment, recognizing your feelings, and moving on without judgment. Mindfulness of how you are approaching your triggers (such as manicured heiresses complaining about part-time help in the garden) and replacing negative thoughts (throwing mud at her) with positive ones (telling her how beautiful her garden is—and *meaning* it) can have a tremendous effect on one's overall sense of contentment.

Building a different habit of mind takes time. It's difficult to let go of our preconceived notions, our assumptions about others, and our anger over perceived injustice, but it's not only possible, it's the only way forward.

My husband and I were convinced that we'd only be in our city house for three years tops. Conversely, we were convinced that we'd be in the country home that we lost for many years.

It's tough to get started, but on the other side of the street from this property is a lot that once looked the same and now grows six thousand pounds of fresh vegetables a year.

We were wrong on both counts. Life doesn't work that way. And it scares me to think that we could have wasted fifteen years of our gardening lives and young, supple joints sitting in a holding pattern waiting for the home and garden that we really wanted. If you stubbornly refuse to come to a place of peace with where you are and treat it as your home, not where you are housed, you are wasting precious time and mentally beating yourself up every day.

You can still have ambitions. You can still work toward your dreams. You can still achieve what you work for, but you must do so whilst fully accepting *what is right now*. Otherwise the quiet forces of negative energy will enervate you, and trust me, you need all the energy you can harness. Forget about steep slopes, noisy roads, heavy shade, or nasty neighbors—this personal barrier is one of the greatest limitations in your path to creating Eden.

EXERCISE 1: ACCENTUATE THE NEGATIVE?

If all that character building seems a little bit overwhelming, then just for a moment you have my permission to be as negative as possible; in fact, I want you to be.

How often does someone tell you to go outside, look around at your surroundings, and list all the things that depress you about it? You read that right. I don't want touchy-feely forced positivity right now, I want the truth—the naked, no-holds-barred truth. But I promise I won't leave you feeling depressed—when we're done, you'll feel energized.

If we gloss over the difficulties with our garden spaces, we don't fool anyone, including ourselves. But more importantly, *we cannot solve these issues*. The successful gardener works within the framework of the space he or she has, understanding it for the challenges and opportunities it presents. Then they must consider options with regards to their resources of money, time, and energy.

But first and foremost we have to open our eyes and be as honest as we can be.

Though there are many factors outside the borders of your property that can indirectly affect you as a gardener (like that neighbor who stares at you from her porch all day, every day), we're going to assume that, by virtue of the fact that you picked up this book, we're all sharing neighborhoods that have their difficulties. Instead of focusing on these, let's deal with the space you own or rent.

Are you dealing with any of the following?

A blank, weedy lot	No sense of a garden
No walkways	House set badly on lot
Steep grades	Poor drainage
Heavy shade	HOA restrictions
No shade	Rental restrictions
Poor, compacted soil	Awkward setbacks
Oddly shaped lot	Chain-link fence
Large, poorly sited trees	No obvious views
No place to eat or entertain	A very small space, period
No fence or other boundaries	

One of our most obvious issues was privacy, and when five new houses were built over three years, I could no longer ignore it. Raising the retaining wall with reclaimed bricks and planting softening shrubs created a patio that directed the eye to a view of the mountains beyond the rooftops.

We've all got challenges—we just need to identify them.

Go on, grab a pencil. You can find your own copy of the following chart on page 200.

Obstacles and Opportunities

Obstacle	Opportunity
A blank weedy lot	
Poor drainage/boggy site	
Large, poorly sited trees	
??	

You've probably thought of some obstacles that I haven't mentioned. That's good. You're trying to be as negative and critical as possible, though with any luck you've also noticed a few things in the process that you actually like. We'll come back to those later. For now, we're dealing with the obstacles that seem overwhelming. Write them down and hold onto that list for Chapter 3.

Right now we've got to hunt down some perspective.

Perspective: The game changer

Over time, we human beings become blind to our personal space. It's the reason why right now, on your kitchen countertop or buffet, there is a semi-permanent pile of months-old shopping flyers, old vitamin bottles, and a houseplant on the critical list. I'm not throwing stones, I've got my own pile. I merely draw your attention to the fact that the same thing happens in the garden. And, quite frankly, it is far easier to blame difficult terrain and greedy shade trees than to look at it one more time with a fresh perspective.

Find a friend

Afraid your eyes have dimmed over time? Maybe it's time to phone a friend. It's a sad fact that we human beings are highly skilled at being critical of one another, but we also have the ability to harness this power for good. A friend that gardens, and gardens well, can be an angel sent from heaven when the budget doesn't include a personal consultation by a top landscape designer.

When I moved into my last home, I despaired at three levels of honeysuckle vines, poison ivy, weedy grass, and groundhog holes, with a few shovelfuls of broken glass and fused coal clinkers thrown in for giggles. The woods were reclaiming the yard, one wild grape tendril at a time, privacy was non-existent, and I had absolutely no idea where to start.

So, I readied my notebook, pulled out some graph paper, and invited a friend over. She had just taken a lot in her own small town and turned it into a gorgeous space where gentle formality paired with soft country plantings, creating a miraculous surprise for anyone who opened her garden gate and peeked inside. I respected her opinion, but didn't hold out much hope. Faced with my hilly topography, carnivorous vines, and greedy trees, I was fairly certain that even the stoutest plantswoman would quail at the challenge.

She didn't. Instead, she said something that stuck with me ever since and inspired much of my garden design over the next few years, "I envy you your levels," she remarked over her wine glass. "You can create so many different rooms in your garden."

Rooms eh? I hadn't thought about that. Instead I had focused on the truncated spaces, the lack of tradi-

The use of archways, old doors, and changes of level created a room effect in my garden, moving the visitor seamlessly from one area to another. Here, the shade garden entrance, which was once occupied by scrubby grass.

tional flat lawns, and general obstacles to a "standard" garden. My friend was challenging me to look beyond the obvious use of the space and create something a little different . . . and that's precisely what I did.

The back garden levels allowed me to create "rooms" for the vegetables and the compost pile, a room for the bees and soft fruit, winding paths and secret steps, and even a room with playhouse and lawn for the children. A long, slender stretch of grass in the front became a sunny perennial border, and that greedy maple provided enough shade to keep potted hosta healthy in a shady room on the north side of the house.

All because someone helped me see it a little differently.

Imagine it naked

I still try to keep my perspective fresh by playing a little game with myself when I visit someone else's intimidating horticultural masterpiece. It's not playing fair I know, but I squint my eyes and try to imagine the space as it once was: naked. Probably plain, possibly difficult. Then I open them wide again, and suddenly I can see the paint separated from the canvas. It's just a little exercise in reclaiming perspective, but it's always wise to keep these skills fresh for the next time I come across a rocky outcropping or an inconvenient tree and need to brainstorm the possibilities.

Just for the record, I do it with intimidating people too.

When you're in a beautiful garden and are told that it has come a long way, ask the owner if they have before pictures to help you understand the space better. Most gardeners cannot wait to share such photos, and you might gain valuable information on how to approach your own naked garden.

The west corner of the lowest level of the garden became a vegetable garden, accessible by stone steps roughly cut into the steep bank.

Be a teenager again

A fresh perspective does not allow itself to be beaten by a laundry list of zoning requirements, tree drip lines, and one inch of topsoil. It bears more than a passing resemblance to the unbridled idealism of a teen—the practicalities will come after the dreams are drawn up.

Right now in my teenage son's life there are nothing but possibilities ahead. Ask him what he wants to do after he graduates from high school and he will tell you with a straight face that he wants to live on a beach in Australia and travel the rest of the world out of a backpack until he's ready to enter academic life again.

"Where will you get the money?" I ask, in my most middle-age moments.

"I'll find a job," he responds, as he shrugs and smirks at me like I'm being unnecessarily cautious.

"But where will you live?" I press on, unable to visualize my cherubic, four-year-old at eighteen, homeless, and begging on the streets of Sydney.

"I'll find a room in a house, Mom," he says. Patting me on the back, he adds, "Geez, all you can see are the obstacles!"

This is not the time to righteously remind him that I did something similar at his age, but it may be the time to remind myself. I saw very few obstacles that could not be overcome at eighteen, and for the most part I overcame them. Time can take its toll on idealistic thinking, but we must remind ourselves that when we stop believing, we stop achieving.

Belief will turn your poorly drained swamp into a wildlife refuge. It will turn your dry hillside into a micro vineyard, and your chain-link fence into a green wall of privacy.

You know your garden's limitations. Now let's go face them.

SMALL SPACE, MANY USES

Karen Birch and Jerry Cayford see their small urban garden perched on a hillside in the middle of town a bit like a theatre stage. Except in this theatre, the curtain is always up, revealing to fellow members of their small mid-Atlantic community how gardening and sustainable methods of permaculture are not only attainable in a small space, but incredibly beautiful.

Jerry, a grocery receiver for a local co-operative market, originally bought the small house as a HUD foreclosure thirteen years ago. His first project was the installation of a magnificent boulder discovered in the woods nearby. Years later, his adoration for this garden anchor is still evident in the words he uses to describe it: "It is a gloriously beautiful rock, maybe a ton and a half, bluestone granite with quartz veins through it, somewhat smoothed, presumably from eons in the Potomac River."

Friends came to help, a walking tripod was erected, a party ensued . . . a memory was imprinted. Not too long afterwards, he started a two-row vineyard on the rocky hillside.

At the time, Jerry was working for an environmental think tank. He had huge plans for the renovation of the dilapidated house and garden—then surrounded by a chain-link fence—but a lot has happened since then.

For one, Karin. A textile artist whose complex and innovative work has graced

omes, businesses, and galleries for decades, Karin moved into the little house with Jerry in 2007, and the garden took off. The chain-link fence was removed, grass was similarly dismissed, and a host of ground covers, perennials, edibles and annuals took their place, introducing neighbors with similar hilly sites to the many ways a sloped garden could be clothed without buying a lawn mower.

But the years brought another change—this one not so welcome. A highly educated man with a gift for writing, Jerry was nonetheless laid off during the 2008 economic crisis and inconceivably found himself without full-time work for the next two years.

The garden in many ways sustained him, providing projects like dry stone walls, flagstone steps, reclaimed brick pathways, and wisteria arbors supported by hand-planed timbers—his hands, his plane. Meanwhile, Karin continued to work tirelessly and imaginatively within the framework of frugality and challenging topography.

Working together in a garden partnership is challenging but satisfying. Karin chooses plants based on color and texture and tends to stay away from fussy species, describing her gardening style as "French Intensive" and Jerry's as "hotter and tropical." And she admits that where Jerry is a man of exacting, big projects, she's not good at planning. "I like it to evolve," she says, pointing to self-seeded verbena that is currently picking up a hint of violet from neighboring sage.

Later we sit with a cup of tea in a front room lined with books and plants and pieces of art that speak of lives led with passion and determination. A nearby woodstove radiates warmth, and I ask them if they'd like a bigger garden someday.

Jerry thinks so. "Working with what we have is an interesting and rewarding exercise of its own, but in a bigger garden there are things I would put in, like a pond, maybe a stone or brick grill . . . a wood-fired brick oven."

Karin agrees, but follows it up with a practical consideration for artists and writers living busy lives: "Honestly, a smaller space means that a half-day of work shapes things up beautifully," she says. "That's hard to beat."

3

ACCESSING YOUR CREATIVITY

"Adversity is the midwife of genius."
—Napoleon

I apologize to those readers who are natural creative trail blazers and only picked up this book to find out what the competition is writing, but I'm going to share a little secret that accounts for about half of your superhero powers:

Being creative is not just about a constant stream of ideas and inspirations, it's about *solving problems*, and all of us do this on a more or less daily basis.

When the table leg is short, you don't pull it off and hand lathe a new one, you put a shim under the leg. That's creativity.

When the kids' toys have outgrown their closet, you grab an old wicker hamper and dump them in. That's creativity.

When you go to buy a new cover for the grill and it's outrageously priced but a retro vinyl tablecloth is cheap, you buy it. That's creativity—and it also looks great.

Tie a frayed piece of hemp rope around it to keep the wind from blowing it off and now you're a creative genius working in a new genre of shabby chic retro!

This gardener tie-dyed flags with vegetable-based dyes, creating a light, airy, and attractive feature that blocks an unattractive view of the buildings beyond.

All you were doing is solving problems, and this is precisely what you will be doing in the garden. Solving problems. After all, necessity is the mother of invention.

This life skill, coupled with the wealth of fabulous garden ideas out there is your set of keys to creating a beautiful, functional garden, but you must also be willing to do two things: copy and study.

Copying: The highest form of flattery

In today's image-driven virtual world, you no longer have to go to the library or a botanical garden to find inspirational ideas to copy. Tomorrow's home and garden TV show stars can't wait to show you how to group pots for best effect, make an outdoor table out of a tree stump, or plant a focal point shrub for wow factor in the landscape.

And you can deliberately, and without regret, copy the hell out of everything they show you. No one's going to judge you. No one's going to revoke your gardener's license or yawn when they come over.

Saw it. Coveted it. Photographed it.

Copied it. (Hypertufa troughs are easy to make—and cheap!)

But there are two downsides to copying.

1. The tendency to feel we need *exactly* the same things to create *exactly* the same result, which can get expensive (not to mention ironic when you are purchasing materials to create a look that someone else created for free.
2. No growth in our gardening (if you'll pardon the pun).

So that's why we must also start . . .

Without studying why something works—why it makes you say "Wow!"—copying soon loses its thrill, and you start feeling like you're inhabiting someone else's garden. For some people that's going to be just fine, but those of us with a gardener's soul naturally want to do more, and believe me, when we want to get better at something, we can.

I cannot draw. At least that's what I thought for twenty-three years until I was forced to endure an archaeological drawing class to complete my undergraduate degree. Who knew that the intense study of technique, principles, and perspective could lead to a portfolio of drawings that would make my naturally talented husband exclaim, "You drew that!?"

Today, I still don't consider myself an artist, but I do know that, if forced to, I can hit the books again and draw something with some degree of realism (as long as it's dead, brittle, and more than two hundred years old). And that took study.

Let's look at this concept applied to the garden

While touring a gorgeous garden in Philadelphia, you are struck by the combination of two plants making up a low edging along a long pathway.

The chartreuse stunner is *Hypericum calycinum* 'Brigadoon', and the silver purple leaves belong to *Heuchera* 'Mint Frost'. Both are expensive perennials, and there is absolutely no way you can afford this kind of edging for your front walkway, yet you've been looking for something more exciting than tufts of liriope at your feet and haven't had a creative flash yet. Time to put the thinking cap on.

Why do they work so successfully together? Let's go beyond the wow factor and study them.

They are both low growing. Both have a similar three-season interest period. The color, texture, and shape of their leaves is very different and provides remarkable contrast.

So, if we are going to copy this idea in another

Hypericum calycinum *'Brigadoon' and* Heuchera x *'Mint Frost' edge a pathway.*

way, we can look for cheaper plants that have low growing habits, grow well during the same season, and whose colors, textures, and leaf shape contrast with one another. To help our burgeoning creative minds think of something, we'll work with relatively the same colors, that way we're more likely to think of something similar.

How about this?

If there is one plant that is cheap, cheerful, and fast growing, it is creeping Jenny (*Lysimachia nummularia* 'Aurea'). We paired its chartreuse, round, crinkled leaves with the purple lanceolate, strongly veined foliage of bugleweed (*Ajuga reptans* 'Chocolate Chip'), another cheap, fast-growing perennial. Buy a pot of ajuga and you can easily divide it into ten to twelve smaller plants; and creeping Jenny is legendary for rooting at its leaf nodes when put directly on moist soil.

So, we copied the general idea of a combination that we loved and couldn't afford, but studied it carefully and applied its design principles to something that we could.

Why garden porn is good

You've probably heard many garden writers refer to "garden porn" or "plant porn" in the last ten years or so. The terms still make me laugh, but boy are they apt. They refer to photos of gardens and garden tableaus that make our mouths hang open and our hands itch to get busy. They can be books, magazines, or websites that inspire us through images. They get the creative juices flowing and the mind and body ready to go.

We just have to be careful that we are using them as triggers of inspiration and not as reminders of deprivation. Sometimes that's a very fine line.

About a thousand years ago, when I was newly on my own and had a very tiny budget, *The Tightwad Gazette*, written by a very smart woman named Amy Dacyczyn, served as my bible. She gifted me with the philosophy of treating tightwaddery as a game, not an

Ajuga reptans 'Chocolate Chip' *pairs brilliantly with* Lysimachia nummularia 'Aurea', *creating a strong statement that doesn't betray how little it actually cost.*

Some of my best ideas have been triggered by the best ideas of others.

exercise in deprivation. She felt that one of the best ways to fight thoughts of deprivation is to immediately cancel all subscriptions you might have to mainstream lifestyle magazines. Mrs. Dacyczyn knew that when faced with all the things a human being could possibly want, it would be near impossible to skim through these magazines and not feel deprived.

I never enjoyed lifestyle magazines anyway, so it wasn't a great sacrifice, but as my second-hand gardening book collection grew and I found myself splurging on a yearly subscription of *Fine Gardening* or *Horticulture* magazine, I wondered why this philosophy didn't apply to gorgeous photos of carrots and roses as much as it did to new shoes and fine furniture.

I didn't feel deprived by those photos and informative plant profiles—I felt inspired. And, yes, there were plenty of ads for insanely beautiful, totally out-of-reach greenhouses or garden sculptures, but overwhelmingly, pictures and articles about growing plants and creating gardens seemed well within reach because *I could grow them.*

You never know what might inspire you to put flowers and objects together. My favorite gin had a hand in this one.

I can't fabricate a seven-hundred-dollar pair of Dolce & Gabbana shoes in my living room, or build a four-thousand-dollar antique cabinet, but I have a very good chance of propagating a coveted hydrangea from a cutting or finding a tree peony at a plant swap—and so do you.

Furthermore, through these photos, we can access grand-scale creativity, study it carefully, and then attempt to create something similar in our own gardens on a far smaller scale.

It would be hard to wander this classic perennial border and not be inspired to create new color and texture combinations the moment you got home.

Why 1 Percent gardens are also good

Thank goodness the gardens of the 1 percent exist. Thank goodness there are those who are wealthy enough to create Eden on a grand scale and make endowments to public botanical gardens.

Yes, I'm saying thank goodness there are people with gardens a hell of a lot better than ours who want to share them with us. Why?

Because whether you tour them or read about them, you are *inspired* by them. An inspired mind is a positive, creative mind; and if you have managed to recognize feelings of envy and resentment for the limiting feelings that they are and moved past them, then you have the power to create your own, unique-to-you garden right now.

You may not be able to create an Italian water garden á la Longwood Gardens in Kennett Square, Pennsylvania, or a desert garden on the scale of Huntington Botanical Gardens in San Marino, California, but you can take elements of these gardens and apply them to your own landscape and benefit from the ideas of expensive designers.

When you don't have a birdbath but you have a strawberry pot.

Do your homework—the best kind

Read. Tour. Copy. Study. Take notes and ask questions in your quest for problem-solving ideas. Pay special attention when you're touring smaller urban gardens, even when they are obviously expensive smaller urban gardens. You may be surprised by the backstory of gorgeous landscapes that were once a major pain in the butt for those who refused to give up and eventually created something beautiful.

EXERCISE 2: OBSTACLES AND OPPORTUNITIES

We're letting go of what we have to have. We're committing ourselves to the space that we're in. We're giving friends a chance to throw out ideas, and we've started playing the naked game with landscapes that intimidate us. And when it comes to solving the major problems with our property, we've learned that we have the tools to access the creative genius of others when we feel we're lacking a little on the genius front ourselves.

Now it's time to look back at that list you created at the beginning of Chapter 2 and start brainstorming your way down the "opportunities" column.

Three thoughts before you begin:

- There are no judgments in brainstorming—anything goes.
- You're not discussing the minutiae of "how," only "what"
- Choose your moment; fill in the blanks when you're feeling the most inspired. Usually after reading, touring, or chatting with other gardeners.

Here are some ideas I came up with (and some I ended up implementing) from a few of the obstacles I listed in Chapter 2.

Obstacles and Opportunities—Solved

Obstacle	Opportunity
A blank, weedy lot	Raised beds in geometric patterns with mulched walkways
Poor drainage/boggy site	A wetlands and wildlife refuge A rain garden
Large, poorly sited trees	Cool shade gardens Tree house
Steep grade	Terraced, Mediterranean garden "Painting" with ground covers
House set badly on lot/oddly shaped lot	Garden rooms
Rental garden	Garden that relies on edible and ornamental annuals

(Continued)

Rental restrictions on planting	Potted garden Annual garden
No obvious views	Sanctuary garden Secret garden
No fence or other boundaries	Mixed tree/shrub screens
No shade	Tree of my choice! Sunny cottage garden
Heavy shade	Fernery Cool patio for entertaining
No place to eat or entertain	Informal gravel patio near house with various containers Bistro table in a corner of the lawn
Poor, compacted soil	Raised beds with rich soil Wildflower meadow
No sense of a garden	Front entrance archway/gate
HOA restrictions	Interesting colors & textures for foundation planting in front Whatever I can get away with in back
Small space	Formal town garden
Chain-link fence	Evergreen neutral screen Annual climbers

So, feeling creative? Feeling inspired? Feeling up to the challenge? Good. Let's take all that positive energy and plan a garden.

CURB APPEAL

Creating a garden next to a wind-swept coastline isn't everyone's definition of ideal. Punishing winds and salt spray are enough to make most people throw down a bit of gravel and focus their spare time on collecting sea glass. But thankfully for passers-by, Louise Handley hasn't let these obstacles stop her from creating a breathtaking garden in her Bandon, Oregon, neighborhood, where shrubs, perennials, and self-seeders spill out onto the street, make people smile, and miraculously turn a city fire hydrant into a piece of installation art.

She and her husband and four children moved to the modest home and lot back in 1976. The house—constructed with everything from driftwood to reclaimed lumber—needed a lot of renovation work, but the garden needed even more.

"Well, there wasn't a garden," says Louise. "Just two very unhealthy shrubs."

It isn't atypical for the neighborhood, or surprising. Cold north winds strike the backyard in the summer, winds from the south hit the front in the winter. So how did the stunning garden I see now come about? "With a windbreak," says Louise with a laugh. "Without a windbreak you can't grow anything." Forty

years later, the couple is often amazed by just how windy it really is when they leave the tranquility of the garden to check the mailbox.

Louise's husband Richard was a schoolteacher, and with four children and limited funds, she perfected the art of propagating plants by old methods handed down from her mother. With the help of a benevolent climate, a huge amount of her starts have survived and thrived, particularly the azaleas that love the climate and now effortlessly mask a chain-link fence.

As we're on the topic, I ask about the fence. This was one of the first features I noticed, but only because my gardener's eye had never seen one clothed so successfully with such an array of plant material. Louise has created a stepped approach with large flowering shrubs and perennials that draw the eye out and down to the street and almost *offer* the garden to the

casual observer. The fence seems to disappear in the beautiful chaos of flowers and foliage.

"In the first five years of our marriage, we moved nine times with my husband's schooling and job," she recalls. "I had a garden in every one of our rentals and always had people asking me why I was going to the trouble for a rented house. Richard and I often drive by some of those places now and see a massive tree I planted or flowers I put in. That's why. It just makes the world a better place."

She's proud of their garden and is thrilled that it has garnered such interest from those who pass by each day or see it on a garden tour. Her hope is that in leading by example, she can inspire others to take trowel in hand and claim their space—whatever it happens to be.

No doubt she's been successful in that goal far more times than she'll ever know.

4
PLANNING YOUR GARDEN

"Heaven always favors good desires."
—Cervantes

It's overwhelming, I understand. No, really, I understand. Just because you wish to spend the rest of your life lightly dusted in soil doesn't mean you feel any aptitude for creating the space in which to do it. In fact, I know that for many of you the moment you turned the page and saw the title of this chapter you instinctively sucked in your breath . . . and held it.

Let it out. You want a beautiful garden, and when you're journeying toward a destination, it's always a plus to know which way to start walking, particularly if you have a limited amount of food and water.

Instead of letting your stomach knot up, let's ease into the process a little differently, breaking it down into two very manageable parts: planning and designing.

Everyone can plan, but most people feel threatened by designing, so first we're going to do what we're good at in this chapter, and then we'll dabble a little with some easy-to-remember, easy-to-implement, and easy-to-afford design elements in the next.

What is planning?
Planning is:

- Asking yourself what you actually want out there. Veggies or flowers? Pond or swing set? Formal or casual? Pool or just a pool boy?
- Prioritizing those wants with regards to your life circumstances.
- Accounting for maintenance and adjusting accordingly.
- Writing it down before you forget.

It's not the big picture—it's the *very* big picture. But don't let it stress you out.

An inviting entrance?

A productive vegetable garden?

Your own fruit trees?

A sunny mixed border?

A colorful shade garden?

A quiet corner for bees?

What do you want?

Fresh eggs on a daily basis?

A place to entertain?

A striking water feature?

Planning now will:

- stop you from mindlessly implementing features you don't really want;
- help you to face difficult areas on your property;
- allow you to recognize resources and materials for future projects; and,
- solidify a sense of process in your gardening.

At the end of the day, planning gives you direction. Do you know how stressful it is to write a book? Very. An author needs an outline. You are the author of your garden, and a garden plan is the outline.

Too much? Too little? Or just right?

There are three ways to approach the planning process:

1. **Not at all—let it evolve!** Many amazing gardens have been created without any kind of master plan, but more often than not, they are created by highly creative spirits that, if they hadn't gone into accounting or mortgage banking to pay the bills, they would have made great garden designers. If you are fairly certain that this is not you, I urge you to consider another way. Having no plan often results in a lot of do-overs, and some of them might be pretty big . . . and expensive.

2. **A place for everything and everything in its place.** I'm going to caution you against this level of planning. Not only does it involve an inordinate amount of graph paper and pencils, if you are new to this game, it can make you a bit inflexible. When you have limited resources, you don't have the luxury of being inflexible. However, if you love to draw diagrams and a brand-new measuring tape gives you a secret thrill, this might be the way for you.

3. **Moving purposely toward a goal.** I think you've figured out by this point that I'm probably going to advocate a middle ground in your planning process. All I'm asking for is an *idea* of what you want to do that goes beyond "over there, something and over here, something else." It's not a total master plan, but it keeps you moving slowly and organically toward a functional, beautiful garden, because you have a good idea of what you eventually want—even if you don't know exactly how you'll get there.

A little bit of paperwork first

You're going to need a journal. I'm not talking about a cloyingly sentimental diary that charts the ways you are inspired by your garden and then results in saccharine sweet poetry. These days that sort of thing is for social media anyway. What you need is a three-ring binder

Your journal is yours—your format, your divisions, your sketches, and your thoughts.

and plenty of cheap filler paper. While you're at it, get some dividers (you'll figure out how to personalize them as you go), and a pad of graph paper for when you're feeling official and/or creative.

Remember the chart from Chapter 2: Obstacles and Opportunities? I've just given you a place to keep it, a place where you might actually look at it again within the context of other issues relevant to your garden.

You can certainly use computer-generated lists and documents, but I urge you to keep the journal itself off your computer. Why? Because a garden journal is as simple as paper and a pencil, and that simplicity is what will allow you to grab it and head out to the garden with it in your hands.

It's that simplicity that will allow you to jot something down on a Sunday when you wanted to keep your computer switched off (yes, I do this), or save a list of plants you got at a lecture, or roughly sketch a new idea on paper without finding your way through a new software drawing program that drains your will to live long before you ever get anything on the screen.

These things have their place, but so does an old-fashioned garden journal. It's your garden book. Let's add to it now by answering questions that will ease us into the planning process.

What do you want from your garden?

Do you have children? Do you intend to include their needs in your landscape?

Don't smirk. This is a valid question for many gardeners who become so obsessed with planting a space that they completely forget to include places for their growing children. Those spaces could include a playset, a simple swing, a tree house or fort, a living teepee of willow wands, or, my favorite, a small raised bed for them to plant themselves.

It's also important to weigh the child factor when it comes to the fragility of your garden. For instance, children love pea gravel. Not to walk on it mind you, but to throw it.

Mulch is a much less interesting alternative for young hands and keeps your blood pressure down.

Do you want vegetables?

Vegetables are the gateway drug into obsessional gardening. To many people, a garden means vegetables . . . and lots of them. And, with the incredible books and websites promoting edible landscaping and permaculture, it's not hard to see the appeal. Such gardening concepts are particularly suited to gardeners in difficult spaces, because much use is made of vertical plantings, and the ornamental aspects of vegetable gardening are used to their best advantage.

Decide what role vegetables will play in your garden, and how much you actually need. For gardeners who love growing vegetables but are dealing with less than six hours of sun a day, some of the leafy and root vegetables can still provide a harvest, but fruiting plants, like tomatoes and peppers, are going to require putting your name down for a community garden plot somewhere sunny. Such things are important considerations in the planning stage.

Nothing (ahem) beats the freshness of just-harvested vegetables.

Do you want flowers?

Who doesn't? Well, actually, there is a great deal of beauty in the alternative—the shapes, textures, and colors of foliage, the structure of trees, the serenity of open space . . . the three extra hours in your week not spent deadheading blooms and tying up flopping daisies.

A profusion of flowers will brighten both outside and inside spaces.

But for those of us who do love the bright sweetness and surprising complexity of flowers, we're willing to go to a lot of trouble to have them.

Perennials and bulbs will give you two to four weeks of bloom, and will (presumably) come back next year. Annuals will exhaust themselves in an orgy of color, and you'll have to buy or start more next spring. Biennials will give you foliage one year, flowers the next, and check out of the game shortly thereafter. With so many to choose from in each category, figuring out what you want is more about how you want to use them.

→ **As constant fodder for inside vases:** You'll want more of a utility bed for cutting blooms and rely on a healthy mix of annuals and perennials.

→ **As a cottage garden entrance:** You'll be able to get away with some of the easiest and cheapest varieties out there.

→ **As statements by the front door:** You might be able to invest a little more in something special.

Do you want a water feature?

If you crave a pond more than anything but have limited space, don't be afraid to make a large pond with surrounding plants the focus of your garden. But if you only desire the feel and sound of water, I urge you to look at other options of small premade pond forms or container water features that complement rather than dominate other features in your garden.

A place to eat or entertain?

This was the very first consideration for us in our last garden, and I think it is for many people who love their friends and love being outside and want those two things to mix liberally. Even if you decide to only have a small bistro table on a bit of raked gravel, you give yourself another option for entertaining.

A storage area or "working yard"

This is an important consideration in every yard, even on a balcony or patio. You need a little room to work and to store equipment. If you have a very small garden, you may need to incorporate it as a feature of the garden as a whole. If you have a larger space, you may be able to squirrel it away behind hedges. These days, people are recognizing the beauty in the tools and objects of a working garden, so don't be afraid to display them.

Set aside a small work area and recognize that there is beauty "behind the scenes," even when it's almost center stage.

Pathways or large open spaces?

If you want a large open space for children, pets, or to turn your very own cartwheels, you are not alone, but the gardener must decide how best to approach this desire based upon their climate and environmental conditions. In many areas of the country a lawn is just not practical or environmentally responsible, so other alternatives to create useful, open space should be considered, such as using gravel or mulch. For gardeners in areas of the country where summer rains are a part of life, mowing a large, open area can almost be a form of self-defense against the quick encroachment of brush and woody invasives.

If you have several levels on your property, you may want to consider making only one of them a traditional lawn so you can indulge your gardener's heart with pathways and beds in the others.

Pets will also need to be considered when it comes to lawns. If you've got a small space and a big dog, I like to advise people to heavily mulch one area of their garden (perhaps under a large tree), specifically for their dog, so their play space is not compromised by browned spots and messy shoes.

Tempted to theme your garden?

Planning your garden around a theme can give you direction, cohesiveness, and a framework upon which to design. Whether it is a tropical paradise, a Mediterranean terrace, a Japanese garden, or an exuberant cottage garden, it's easier to fit pieces together and to instantly know when an object or plant is not going to work.

You may also wish to apply a theme to a small part of your space, but if you do so, it is best to work with a part of the garden that is somehow set apart from the rest of your garden with natural or artificial boundaries.

Wildlife sanctuary

If you are not heavily planting your garden for production, it is a great pleasure to watch wildlife use it for water, food, and shelter, particularly during the winter months. A garden (or part of a garden) planted with these needs in mind can be remarkably low maintenance, but don't kid yourself that it's "no maintenance."

If you have a low swampy area in your yard, this is precisely what you should be focusing upon instead of wasting all that energy on figuring out how to sue the developer.

Planting for pollinators is increasingly popular these days and a win-win proposition.

Adapting and prioritizing

Our desires must obviously be matched and adapted to our life circumstances, our budget, and our energy level. These factors change over time, some for the better (money), some for the worse (energy). The list you have made based on the above questions should be prioritized to reflect your circumstances right now, but you should also be open to future changes.

Let's look at an example.

John and Julie have young children and are living on a suburban lot on one income. Their idea of a great evening is a home-cooked meal with great ingredients and friends coming over to share it. They love flowers and water features and have been thinking about a cottage garden, but realize that it won't add much to the home economy and will require a fair amount of maintenance. They'd also love to pick their own apples from the comfort of the backyard and really want to screen their neighbor's ugly chain-link fence.

After going through their list they decide that their biggest priority is a lawn for the kids and a seating area where they can watch them as well as entertain friends. As they don't want to be watched themselves, they will immediately plant the fence line with a fast-growing broad-leafed evergreen. A large vegetable garden for fresh ingredients is also a priority, and they decide to have one bed devoted to cutting flowers as well as incorporating edibles in other parts of the landscape.

A water feature is not a great idea with small children running around, so that will be shelved for later, when the lawn has been outgrown, and perhaps at that time they can think about putting in a larger pond. Meanwhile they can indulge their love of the sound of water with a container fountain near the seating area, where they can also indulge their love of flowers with various ornamental pots.

As you work through your own list, and prioritize your wants and needs, think in terms of stages of the garden and stages in your life. It's okay if you don't think you'll be there another five years. Maybe you will be and maybe you won't be. Give yourself a plan that stays flexible in the face of uncertainty.

The maintenance factor

In my opinion, the biggest pitfall in planning one's garden is not honestly accounting for the amount of maintenance that you can devote to upkeep. Whether you are a millionaire creating a showpiece botanical garden with four staff gardeners too few, or a man with two vegetable beds and four hours too few, to ignore this consideration is to always feel one step behind and never allow the garden to be what you imagined it to be, and that's not a pleasant feeling.

So, as we work our way through our plans for the garden, we must, and I repeat, MUST be truthful with ourselves and with the amount of maintenance our garden will demand of us.

You don't have unfettered access to garden staff. You're going to have to work out there. But if you want to work a little less, *you might want to rethink the following choices carefully.*

- Planting climbers, such as roses, wisteria, grapes, trumpet vine, climbing hydrangea, Virginia creeper, Boston ivy, and English ivy.
- Planting anything that relies on pest or disease control in order to fruit successfully (in my climate, grapes and peaches).
- Planting anything that needs supplemental watering after the first year and for the rest of its life.
- Planting anything that re-seeds itself in your climate and whose seedlings are tenacious, such as Northern sea oats and lemon balm in the East, locust and pampas grass in the West, or honeysuckle and mimosa in both.
- Planting anything that spreads aggressively through underground stolons, such as St. John's wort or rice paper plant.
- Garden beds with visible edges (rather than low-growing plants creating soft edges).

This stunning rambling rose and clematis pairing was the highlight of my spring garden for many years, but eventually it became a maintenance nightmare and was removed and replaced with a smaller climbing rose that could behave itself and didn't require me to pull out a ladder three times a year.

- Long borders filled with perennials that need deadheading, cutting back, and dividing.
- Choosing plants that are not recommended in your hardiness zone and need wrapping, etc., to make it through winter.
- Hedges planted in tight spots, which makes trimming mandatory.
- Semi-tropical plantings that require digging in your climate.

Does this mean you can't have the rambling rose or perennial border? Of course not. However, you must be sure that you have the ability, and desire, to give more time to these garden features. Every winter I tenderly dig out cannas and colocasias because I love them. I can't be bothered to do the same for a gladiola.

For a harder-hitting look at what you should be thinking about when it comes to maintenance, I urge you to disobey all rules of book reading and skip ahead to Chapter 9; just make sure you come back.

EXERCISE 3: SKETCHING OUT A *VERY* ROUGH IDEA

Ever grabbed a napkin and sketched out a quick design for something you knew you'd forget later? That's all I'm going to ask you to do now, minus the napkin. I'm sure in many snobby horticultural circles I will be ostracized for the casual nature of the next exercise, but I'm aware of something they may have forgotten in their climb up the green ladder: most everyday gardeners do not have the desire or the energy to do much more than sketch out a rough plan.

1. Grab a piece of graph paper so you have lines to work with and use a pencil to sketch a rough outline of your property boundaries from a bird's-eye view. If you want to be a little more exact, find out your property measurements (for example, fifty by one hundred twenty-five feet) and scale it to fit your graphing paper. Once you are satisfied, go over the line with a black fine-point marker. Make a couple photocopies in case of mistakes made in the next step.
2. Now, use your best guess to place the outline of your house where you feel it sits on your property. Again, when you are satisfied, outline it in black marker and make some copies.
3. Next you will sketch major (as in non-removable-with-your-budget) features. A large tree or a brick wall are examples of this. Remember, you're working from a bird's-eye view, so a tree should be a large circle, not an actual tree with trunk. Outline these in black too.
4. Make several copies of this final sketch, hole punch them, then put them in your journal.

There are two ways I like to use this rough drawing in my planning. Either I use a piece of tracing paper over the top and sketch ideas that can be overlaid one on top of another, or I make lots of photocopies and just draw directly on the sketch itself.

If I want to focus on a specific area of the garden, I'll do the exact same thing, just magnified without the house and property. When doing this I'm much more likely to take a few measurements to make sure my desires don't outstrip my available space.

You don't need to know the universal sign for a staircase or be able to draw perfect triangles. Pretend you're just drawing on a napkin and try. Look at your list and start to sketch a few of your desires, keeping in mind the terrain, and with a basic idea of shapes relative to the scale of the house. Think of it as putting puzzle pieces together. You're not putting in specific plants or design elements, you're just getting an idea of how the features you want can flow together. If you mess up, throw it away and try again.

Congratulations, you just made a plan

A drawing without decent measurements. Yes, it's heretical. Yes, I'll have to hide my face in certain horticultural circles. But it's also real life. If we want to plan our gardens, we need something that's accessible and easy, and my experience is that most great ideas start on some version of a napkin anyway.

In case you're still not convinced, here's an example of the sketch I did at my last house about two years after we moved in (already having made a few additions like vegetable beds and a brick patio), and a rough sketch of where everything ended up eight years later and I needed a map for garden tours.

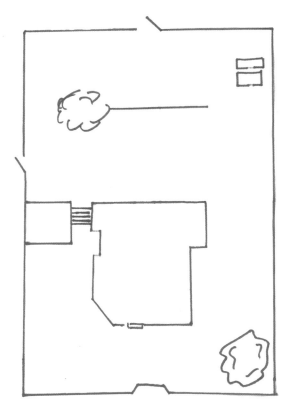

First property sketch.

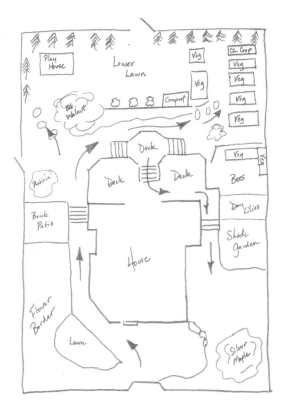

Final property sketch.

It may be rough, it may be flexible, it may bear little relationship to the final sketch you make of your garden someday, but you've given yourself a road map.

Now let's start driving.

A TOWNHOUSE TRANSFORMED

As I knock on Amy Hebert's door, I realize I haven't checked the number plate to make sure I'm in the right place. I smile to myself and glance briefly at the gold numbers, but it's unnecessary. After all, I'm looking for the home of a gardener, and no other home on this block of Northern Virginia townhomes draws visitors to the door the way this one does.

Perhaps it's the stately magnolia or the burnished bark of the crepe myrtle, but as I wait for my hostess to open the door I feel the graceful, dignified charm of a Southern garden surrounding me.

An elegant iron urn sits sentry at the entrance, planted with clematis and trailing vinca. Wisteria climbs the columns supporting the balcony and falls softly down from the iron railings above. Amy opens the door and greets me, and the sound of her gentle Southern accent completes the scene.

Certainly she and her husband are a long way from their extended family in Louisiana, but a lay-off eight years ago forced them to consider jobs farther north, ending in the purchase of a townhome

that bears little resemblance to the land and home they sold to make the move.

Not gardening the tiny space was never an option for Amy. It's in her blood—and so is adapting to change of circumstance. Seventy-five years ago, Amy's grandparents and their seven children (including Amy's mother) were transported to Arkansas from their home in California and interred in a Japanese-American camp for three years.

At the end of the war, her grandparents stayed in the South and built a successful nursery business, which her uncle then turned into a fifty-four-acre botanical garden just outside of Baton Rouge named Imahara's.

"That's my mother's side of the family, but really, gardening is on both sides. My father was crazy about his vegetables—they were his passion," says Amy.

She and her siblings grew up helping in the garden, canning the harvest, and coming to love a life that revolved around the bounty and beauty of plants. Amy continued to garden as she rented apartments and houses on her own, and then later with her husband Chris and their son, Ethan.

Moving into a townhouse was yet another challenge. Poor, compacted soil made planting difficult and required yards of bagged compost and garden soil. The back "garden" was little more than a muddy passageway to the garage and contained HVAC equipment and the main electrical box. Amy knew she wanted a garden that reflected her Southern roots—a garden that was part of the home, not separate from it.

Six years later, a deck seating area is beautifully visible from the home's sitting room, and stepping stones "mortared" with creeping herbs lead you back to the garage and another wisteria arch. Amy's pots and New Orleans-style urns—some of which she's had longer than she's been married—are everywhere.

For a busy couple who work full time, it's just enough garden to enrich their life without becoming onerous, though Amy's got big plans for her retirement garden someday.

"A tiny house and huge garden!" she laughs with excitement, and I realize that this gardener views starting over again as an opportunity.

Her grandparents would be very proud.

SECTION TWO
ACHIEVE

5
TACKLING GARDEN DESIGN

"Our doubts are traitors and make us lose the good we oft might win by fearing to attempt."
—William Shakespeare [*Measure for Measure*]

I have nothing but awe for the landscape designers and architects who can create beauty with a few scribbles of their magic pens, but I'm not one of them, and chances are neither are you. Good design might take us a little more time, but I truly believe it's achievable.

Designing a garden is a humbling experience when you're not a garden designer. It's a particularly humbling experience when you're on a budget and you have a difficult space. Constrained as we are by money, time, and energy, a design that might be the work of a moment to the Martha Stewarts of this world is a teensy bit harder for the likes of us.

We want color! We want texture! We want an excess of joy! Bottom line, we want a garden that says, "The person who lives here must have paid someone tens of thousands of dollars to create this masterpiece. Except they didn't, so they must be a genius."

A tall order.

So we head down to the library, check out fifteen books on design, come home, open the first one up . . . and feel overwhelmed. Graph paper? Triangulation? Drawing to scale? Good Lord, all we wanted to do was plant stuff, and now we feel like middle-schoolers struggling in math class.

A few stalwart souls will dutifully pull out the graph paper and head outside with a measuring tape (these are the overachievers you sat next to in calculus). But, sadly, too many will mentally shut down in the face of all that paperwork and consider the job too daunting. It is to *those* gardeners that I dedicate this chapter.

I understand your fear. I have stood in front of a naked bed (not the other way around), and felt that every choice I made would be scrutinized and found wanting. I have leafed through countless two-dimensional design plans and found nothing to inspire me to create my own. I've read good design books and bad design books, and felt inadequate as I tried to ingest the many aspects of designing a gorgeous garden.

And then I put the books aside and just got started.

Trying to figure out the what and where can be exhausting.

I am not discounting the excellent work of many authors out there, nor am I asserting that the finer points of garden design are irrelevant or nitpicky—they're not. I am merely recognizing that analysis paralysis is the result of too much information too quickly, especially in a discipline where you already feel a little vulnerable.

I can't tell you how to design your garden, but I can give you basic guidelines that will provide you with a starting point on this slightly terrifying journey and perhaps encourage you to see your space in a different way. These tips will guide you as you consider your budget, time, and energy, and give you a framework so you can recognize resources when you see them, preventing you from wasting money on plants and objects that don't really contribute to your garden as a whole.

I have identified those that have helped me the most in the past and grouped them loosely into six categories: containers, garden beds, pathways, seating areas, views, and accessorizing.

Plus, experts have contributed their top design tips, and you will find them throughout the chapter.

Once these fundamental guidelines are under your belt, I urge you to further continue your studies into the tenets of design. Who knows, it may just become one of your favorite subjects. It certainly has become one of mine.

⁓

First, a few general thoughts applicable to the entire design process, which will hopefully allay some stomach-churning fears.

Gardening is a process, and each stage takes time

If nothing else stays with you from reading this book, I hope it will be this simple truth: an instant garden soon becomes a boring garden, as does an instant design. In many ways, the

Gardens installed all at once often lack a gardener's touch.

Tackling Garden Design

budget-constrained gardener is given a better opportunity to grow with his garden than his wealthier counterpart. It's the joy of watching things become, rather than watching them be.

Embrace the small steps the garden forces you to take and the little miracles it chooses to let you see as a result of that pace. If you're moving slowly, you're not only able to adapt your design to a new situation ("Honey, I'm pregnant!"), but you also gain the courage to make those changes as your skill levels increase.

Don't be afraid to move plants, and then move them again

My gardening sister does not consider herself a garden designer, just a really good mover. Consequently, the gorgeous pathway and entrance to her deck has undergone more than four major renovations, but makes her look like she's got a gift. She does: the gift of a good back.

You're going to lose time this way, and some plants resent you for moving them around, but without the benefit of academic or designer experience, learning from your mistakes is a great teaching tool.

If something is bothering you about the design, chances are it's not right

We all doubt ourselves, but most of us know what the problem is, even if we don't know how to solve it. If you don't trust your own instincts, trust those of a gardening friend. Ask them to look at the design and tell you what the flaws are. If you're on the same page, it's time to rip something out and try again. Asking for some ideas may only cost you a glass of wine, some munchies . . . and your pride, but it's worth it.

Take chances

You are not growing as a gardener and designer if you are sticking with the same ideas, the same arrangements, and the same accolades. The point is to get better. Yes, there's going to be someone who doesn't like your design, but you must consider their opinions and decide whether they are worth listening to. If they are, then listen.

Don't get discouraged

Hitting what you perceive to be your own limits of creativity is a humbling experience, but despite my previous flippancy, it is precisely the catalyst you need to push you to the next level. Put down your shovel and come back to your project with fresh eyes and fresh energy. You're creating a beautiful space out of a difficult space—and you're doing it on your own. It's tough work; be kind to yourself.

Now, let's look at a few fundamental design categories and some of the guidelines I have found most helpful over the years.

Basic guidelines: Containers

Containers add interest to doorsteps, patios, and the garden itself, but they can just as easily look awkward, tired, and shabby, particularly when you cannot afford better or larger pots and have a disparate collection. Keep them *fed*, keep them *watered*, and apply a few of the following design tips.

When it comes to containers, the only limit is your imagination.

Grouping for effect

The whole is greater than the sum of its parts. Pots and objects grouped together and height-staggered with bricks, risers, or upturned pots make a stronger statement than those that are spaced out awkwardly. This is also true for plants within containers,

THE PROS WEIGH IN

Julie Moir Messervy, Landscape Architect
Julie Moir Messervy Design Studio

- Create multiple outdoor rooms for different activities. Even a very small property can have several clearly defined zones.

- Create "visual breathing room" around important objects in your landscape. Whether it's your house, a significant tree, or a water feature, objects need some space around them. I tell people to imagine that their house has fallen forward onto its façade—that imprint is usually just the right amount of room needed for a level lawn, patio, or garden.

- Resist the urge to buy every plant you love. Edit your favorites down to just a few, and plant them in masses and swathes. Not every plant has to look its best in every season, but there should be a couple standouts at all times, so there's always something beautiful to capture the eye.

plants within beds, and small tchotchkes around the garden. If you insist on a collection of garden gnomes, then for pity's sake, group them.

Grouping these colorful mushrooms with a ceramic gnome makes a fun, powerful statement—far more than placing them here and there.

Thriller, spiller, filler

You've heard the phrase, but what does it mean? When planting a container, choose taller anchor plants for height, plants with trailing stems to spill over the edges, and plants to provide body and fullness to the pot. Think in terms of height graduation and slight asymmetry as you plant. There is nothing worse than a spiky cordyline sitting bang in the middle of a pot with the first filler a good ten inches below, especially two months after it was originally planted. Foliage color and texture are your friends—contrast them and make your containers pop.

Use those square inches of soil

Plant spacing guidelines go out the window when it comes to container arrangements, but you must be prepared to feed them regularly during the growing season to account for competing roots. Stuff those pots with plants, and if you can cut holes in the side of a basket or container, then stuff a few in there too.

This container relies on stunning foliage and contrasting textures, all in graduating heights. No flowers required.

Make a statement with a container water feature

Container water features, either with or without pumps, are still novel enough to make your deck or patio special. They don't need to be big, but with the aid of surrounding potted plants will make a big impact. Even a large bowl on a table will do.

If you've got plastic, paint it

There are wonderful colors of spray paint for plastic these days, and one can is enough to transform your tired and shabby plastic pots and (bonus) keep them out of a land-fill. Pick a couple of contrasting colors and then group

Container water features don't necessarily need a pump, nor do they need much space.

the result and you'll be amazed at the statement it makes.

Basic guidelines: Garden beds

Your spade is sharpened, but where to put it? Take a deep breath and believe in yourself.

Connect your space—don't disconnect it

When placing garden beds, beware of the tendency to install "disembodied" beds that have no sense of connection with the rest of the garden. If it's part of a multiphase plan or hiding an eyesore, that's one thing, if it's just "making a bed somewhere," avoid the temptation and use your energy to create something connected to another feature in your landscape.

Use an old hose or marking tape to outline prospective beds

You've only got so much energy. Don't waste it on digging something that doesn't work. Outline your idea for a bed with a hose or orange marking tape, and then let it sit for a day or two while you look at it from several angles. Chances are you're going to make some adjustments, but since you didn't dig first, they'll be easy to make.

Don't overcomplicate your edges

In the zeal to create something different, gardeners often swing wildly in the wrong direction. A gentle curve or two is wonderful if the space calls for it, but sometimes the simplicity of a straight line

THE PROS WEIGH IN

Cheryl Corson, Landscape Architect
Cheryl Corson Design, LLC

- Care for your existing trees and plant new ones early on. This gives them a head start as you develop the rest of your garden plan.

- When planting mixed shrubs, plant with ample space based on their mature spread. Wait five years and you'll be rewarded with irreplaceable form and character. Until they grow in, consider perennial plantings that will eventually become unnecessary as your shrubs mature.

- Learn about perennial plant combinations in pairs. Starting simple is best: Siberian iris bloom together with peonies, heuchera bloom together with penstemon, etc. Once you have some great pairs under your belt, you can study and implement more complex perennial groupings.

works better. And no matter what, stay away from scallops—remember, you've got to maintain those edges.

If you're using straight lines, take measurements

It's a terrible feeling to realize that the boxwood line you've been digging all day is actually a boxwood stagger. Straight lines in the garden call for measurements, preferably made at equal intervals from a permanent structure, such as a house or wall. Time for a little geometry—no worries, you can do it!

Garden rooms are a clever way of making more from less

When there are surprises around yet another corner, the mind stops thinking in terms of square footage and starts thinking in terms of experience. Accentuate natural bends and boundaries in the landscape with plantings to create your own multiroom garden mansion.

Think of bones, flesh, and makeup

Bones are the strong lines in the garden that give it permanence throughout the seasons and can be living or nonliving. If you can't afford a fieldstone wall or 15-foot garden sculpture, evergreen plantings will give you that gravitas in time. Add some flesh in the form of perennials or biennials, and then tart it all up with the seasonally colorful makeup of annuals and you'll have a garden that makes you smile even in the dead of winter.

The rule of three

When planting perennials and annuals, try to plant in drifts of three or five and think in terms of little triangles as you space them. Avoid squares or straight lines or, heaven forbid, circles. For whatever reason, this just works, and somehow makes more out of less.

Lines won't be straight without accurate measurements. Grab the tape!

Plantings strategically block the visitor's view, creating a sense of mystery as to what's under the arbor or around the corner.

After three growing seasons, these perennials have grown together in a pleasing, natural way and do not betray the original planting pattern.

Repetition is key in creating a cohesive garden on a budget

When you're on a budget, the fact is, plants often arrive at your house in the singular, even though you wanted three or five. Using a larger plant or shrub repetitively throughout the garden can help unite all these little elements, as can a strong, repetitive color.

The repetitive use of autumn fern in this entrance planting provides a cohesive framework for other, smaller plants.

THE PROS WEIGH IN

Carolyn Mullet, Garden Designer
Carex Garden Design

- When you have established where you are planting, add plants using this helpful mantra: little, more, a lot. First, choose your garden stars—the specimens. This might be a tree, shrub, or cactus. Add only a few (the "little"). To use more would diminish their impact.

- Next, choose the plants that will give your garden energy and pizzazz. Arrange them in groups of three, seven, or twelve (the "more"). These might be groups of flowering shrubs, textural succulents, or colorful perennials.

- Last, choose plants that will connect all the other plantings together and use "a lot" of each of them. These plants are usually called ground covers and hide all the soil and mulch, making your garden feel lush, lovely, and inviting.

Foliage above flowers

With the exception of annuals, most plants and trees in the garden have a two- to four-week season of bloom. That's a lot of downtime. Planting for all seasons means a good use of flower color with equal (or more) weight given to the color and texture of the foliage. A warning: once you get started in the wonderful world of foliage, you may get rid of flowers completely.

Contrast separates good gardens from great gardens

Don't wait too late in your gardening life to start using the contrast of height, texture, color, and shape to the best advantage in your garden. If you spend time looking at designs in other gardens with this concept in mind, you'll soon start to understand why one garden shines where another merely twinkles.

Begonia is a staple of public gardens, but when you add a bit of contrasting variegated ginger, suddenly this planting pops.

Basic guidelines: Pathways

You've got to get from one part of your garden to another. If you don't create pathways, someone you live with will, and it may not be pretty. As you create rooms and beds, always think about access.

A straight path is often a boring path

A path with a curve or two visually elongates the distance between two points, but be careful, your well-traveled paths (such as the one from the car to the front door) are best kept simple to prevent more convenient paths being created by impatient visitors.

Think about soggy feet

Create your pathways with a slight rise in the center to allow for runoff during rainstorms. If you're investing in a more expensive paving material, you should do it right with a sand and gravel base.

This path could have made a straight beeline for the deck entrance. Instead, a slight bend creates another garden bed and more visual interest.

Match your path material to your environment

In a woodland? Use hardwood mulch or chipped pallets. Cottage garden feel? Pea gravel or beaten earth. Modern, minimalistic space? Add concrete pavers between gravel. Above all else, try to stay consistent. If you don't have enough cast-off bricks to make more than six square feet of pathway, consider working with something else rather than creating a material mishmash.

Give your pathways elbow room

Believe it or not, a wider path does not visually subtract from the garden it traverses, it actually creates the illusion of space. It also makes it possible for friends to walk side-by-side, wheelbarrows to have breathing room, and children to have no excuse for walking on your brick edgings.

Give your pathways destination points

A small tree, a large ceramic container, a doorway to another part of the garden—destination points near the end of pathways draw the eye and, consequently, draw the visitor through your garden.

Basic guidelines: Seating areas

What is a garden if not a place to sit and reflect? Provide seating, but think about the following:

A bench can function as garden art, but the view needs to be artful too.

Siting your bench or chair is about two perspectives: the bench observed, and the bench occupied. Chairs that face an unpleasant view will never be used, so either create a better view or move the chair. I don't care how pretty it is to look at.

Keep a dining area convenient

If you're lugging five trays' worth of food and wine to a back corner of your lot, however beautiful, it probably won't see guests that often. Start with a convenient dining area and create a supplemental space if you still feel the need.

Using contrasting colors of wood chips in this shade garden has cleverly demarcated the pathway whilst blending naturally with the surrounding woodland.

A red chair and potted aspidistra give weight to the bend in this lovely woodland path.

Here, tall verbena (Verbena bonariensis) *pairs with pink muhly grass* (Muhlenbergia capillaris) *to create a soft, monochromatic planting scheme around a simple wooden bench.*

Tackling Garden Design

Use a small side table and two chairs in unexpected places

This creates an intimate seating area around a certain view or a quiet spot. Remember, your guests might need your example to use it, so grab a pitcher of lemonade and some glasses and guide them to experience your garden in a different way.

Basic guidelines: Views

We create views when we create a garden. Period. It's just a question of what they are. Redefine the term "view" for yourself and your guests; it's not all about sweeping plains and majestic mountains.

Expand or contract the view with screening

If you're on the top of a hill, planting clipped evergreen hedges on a property border can draw the eye further up, away from neighboring roof-tops or windows. On the bottom of a slope the same screen can enclose the view to create an intimate, cozy space.

Borrow the views of others

Just because you don't own it, doesn't mean you can't use it. Have a subdivision house up against a field? Draw the eye with a planted corridor heading into the infinity of open space. Love the beautiful shed your neighbor just created in her garden? Don't let your plantings obscure the view, frame it instead.

Force the eye where you want it

Don't worry, it's not painful for your guests, they'll never even know you're doing it. Use

Don't just think about sunshine when setting up seating areas. Use your shady spots—you'll be glad you did.

You might not own the mountains, but with strategic planting, you can use them as a backdrop.

plants or objects as focal points in the landscape to move the gaze further along, to block a difficult view, or to give a sense of destination.

Basic guidelines: Accessorizing

Some people are purists, but others like a bit of "garden jewelry." Just don't go too far and literally gild the lily.

Be deliberate

Know the statement you're making with garden art or ornaments. If you don't know, chances are, neither will anyone else.

Be original

If you love gazing balls, why use them like everyone else sitting next to a bench or on a pedestal? Float them in a bowl or pond, hang them from a tree, arrange several in gravel. Think outside the box with *all* your garden ornaments.

In a quiet corner of this English garden, a floating terracotta hippo brings a memory of time spent in Africa to a small pond.

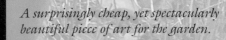

A surprisingly cheap, yet spectacularly beautiful piece of art for the garden.

Be creative

With a bit of spray paint, the craziest things can become garden art. Use cast-off, seat-less chairs painted a bright color to stake flopping perennials. Paint an old rusty bike, wheels and all, and prop it against a fence with flowers growing out of the basket. The possibilities are endless, and when creativity wanes, websites and apps like Pinterest and Instagram are only a click away.

When a little more help is needed

It's going to happen. You're going to hit your Waterloo at some point in your garden design. When it happens, don't panic. Just try to figure out where the problem is so you can ask for specific help from gardening friends, or . . .

Independent Garden Centers

Independent garden centers are one of our most precious resources as gardeners. They are owned and operated by people who love plants, often know a great deal about design, and want you to love your plants too. They can also give you some pointers about how to plant and where to plant, but a caveat is needed here: don't take a picture of your entire backyard and put it in front of a busy nursery grower to plan. She's liable to bite you. Instead, figure out the precise problem you're having and ask for some pointers instead. When she sees that you are actively trying to solve problems instead of just asking for solutions, she'll be happy to

THE PROS WEIGH IN

Jay Sifford, Garden Designer
Sifford Garden Design

- **Embrace juxtaposition.** Consider four plant characteristics: size, shape, color, and texture. Closely matching two of these parameters while varying the other two gives your garden a professionally designed look.

- **Celebrate imperfection.** The Japanese have done this for centuries. Prune that overgrown juniper into a wind-blown focal point, plant moss in the crack of that throw-away ceramic pot, or embrace that eyesore of a tree stump by wrapping it with copper coil tubing.

- **Look for magic in the mundane.** There's magic all around us if we only open our eyes to nature's splendor and possibilities. For instance, celebrate the shafts of sunlight that pierce the woodland canopy each morning by planting a patch of chartreuse sedge in its path as a testimony to its magic.

help. And, for goodness sake, buy some plants—it's the least you can do for a little help in the design department.

Buy a tree, get a consultation

Since nurseries are trying to sell trees (and invested in those trees doing well), you can usually consult with staffers for the best place to site the tree or trees you are buying from them. Don't be afraid to ask questions, but don't expect them to design the rest of your garden too.

Pay for a design consultation

You may not be able to have a designer working side by side with you each day, but you may very well be able to pay for a one- or two-hour consultation to get ideas of what to do in your landscape, or even to draw up a plan.

It's best to discuss the particulars of budget over the phone so you don't end up with a designer discussing 1 percent ideas with a 99 percent budget. Be prepared, take notes, and ask questions. If some of the ideas are still out of your range, ask them to consider something less complex, and don't be embarrassed, just be straightforward.

Sometimes inspirational design ideas come directly from Mother Nature.

THE DIGITAL AGE IS HERE TO HELP

For gardeners who feel they need a bit more guidance and are tech-savvy, there are exciting interactive options out there.

Renowned designer Julie Moir Messervy's new app, The Home Outside® Palette, helps the homeowner approach the big picture of design with a little help from her award-winning firm of landscape architects and designers for free. Here she shares tips for getting the most out of the app:

- Study your *actual* and *ideal* sites. By studying the conditions on your property, you'll have a clear picture of the actual site—what you want to keep and what you want to change. From there you can start to imagine your ideal site using the images, preferences, and ideas you already have of what you'd like to see happen on the land around your house.

- Consider the big moves. Once you understand your actual and ideal sites, you can begin to organize the spaces around your house using one or more big moves. You can choose from four basic layouts: Immersed or Exposed, Central Clearing, House Front and Center, and Open-Air Rooms; select one of three arrangements—All Lined Up, On the Angle, or Voluptuous Curves; or identify a theme by determining a style, naming your property, or dreaming a big idea that pulls together your thinking about what you want your property to become.

- Don't forget to create gathering and getaway zones in your backyard. The place where we most like to live outside is the backyard. Creating places to gather and others to get away will ensure that everybody's needs can be met.

Tackling Garden Design

6

RECOGNIZING RESOURCES

"Cannot people realize how large an income is thrift?"
—Cicero

When surveying my last garden, the casual visitor could be forgiven for thinking we had spent a fortune on hardscaping materials. Thousands of antique bricks and hundreds of large stones made up the walls, walkways, and edgings, and these, along with iron trellises, wood arbors, and various pieces of garden furniture, made it look like I wasn't being totally honest when I insisted that we lived on a tight budget and I made my own yogurt to save money.

I was. What the visitor did not know was that, while the yogurt was setting up, I rescued the bricks from the town dump, hauled stones out of a developer's excavation, and knew how to use a can of spray paint when dealing with discarded furniture. Most of my plants were trades, freebies, or propagations, and I regularly scanned the clearance racks at local big box centers for interesting plants I didn't want to spend a huge amount of cash on.

My garden wasn't completely free. Early on in the planning process, we decided that a fence was necessary for pets and children and put a small part of our home improvement budget toward a professional installation. We built our own deck in stages, as money and time became available over the course of a couple of years. But both of these projects were made possible because we saved money on everything else by recognizing opportunities when they appeared.

Why buy a framework for protective netting when useful materials are lying around in the woods?

Resources to create a beautiful garden are everywhere—you just need to know how to recognize what is sometimes right under your nose.

To help you in your acquisition of wonderful materials, I've put together a few guidelines as well as ideas of where to look for the useful, the whimsical, the practical, and the beautiful.

Operation Freebie—Do's and Don'ts

DO:

Strike while the iron is hot and you won't miss out.

If you see a patio table and four chairs at the end of a driveway that may work for your new seating area and save you hundreds, don't let the fact that you have three kids and groceries in the back of the van stop you from swiftly acquiring it. Though I draw the line at leaving the kids on the side of the road and replacing them with the furniture, it's

Older chaise lounges are often better-made than their modern counterparts. These cheap yard sale finds required only a wire brush and a can of bright spray paint.

certainly possible to knock on a door, contact the owners, and assure them you'll be right back with your neighbor's truck . . . or a swiftly emptied van.

Let people know you're "in the market"

Letting others in your community know that you're looking for all things garden means they will think of you before they throw out that shovel, or a wheelbarrow full of daisy divisions, or the terracotta pots they are tired of heaving out of the shed every spring.

Don't be afraid to ask

When your friend finishes a building project and has lumber left over. When a developer excavates a nearby lot and uncovers the mother lode of building stone. When you pass a tree company chipping branches into mulch. *Ask*. They may have other uses for those materials, but, then again, they may be thrilled that someone else can use them.

Be a little picky—but not too picky

When you're dealing with a small space, the last thing you need is junk sitting around waiting for you to find a use for it. This is why we spent so much time in Chapter 4 planning your garden. If you have a good idea of what you need, it's just a question of deciding if a particular free resource can be used or adapted for that purpose. Though it does happen, you're very rarely going to find exactly what you're looking for, so don't pass up a perfectly good pile of bricks just because you were looking for rust red and they happen to be burnt sienna.

DON'T:

Take without asking

Particularly plants. You'd think this was pretty basic, but sadly it needs to be said. The great English plantsman Christopher Lloyd (who suffered from increased plant losses in his garden as the years went on) admonished the professional plant rustler best when he said, "Do be good about respecting other people's property." We giggle about plant rustling—and I myself have been guilty of a coleus "pruning" or two in the past—but in the end, it comes down to whether or not you are in some small way depriving those whose livelihood depends on their gardens.

Again. *Ask*. The plants/seeds/cuttings over which you are lusting might be for sale in their nursery in order to support their garden. If not? Well, gardeners are generous folks, asking kindly for a clipping might just endear you to the staff.

Gardeners love to find good homes for their plants.

As for all the other stuff, if it doesn't have a "free" sign on it, hunt down someone you can ask. Yes, you might miss out on one or two things, but at least you'll do so with integrity.

Accept plant divisions without offering to help dig them up

This is a little pet peeve of mine. (My friends just read that and thought "Hmmm . . . this is awkward.") Digging is hard work. If you want free plants, be prepared to help in their acquisition. I have a friend that would sooner die than let anyone dig in her garden (she's a little OCD that way), but you can be sure I offer my labor every time (she's got some great plants!).

Keep taking without giving

Healthy relationships are not one-sided. If you have a gardener friend who is giving you tons of divisions every season, think of something you can give them in exchange, like a bottle of wine, or an hour of your time (or a quart of homemade yogurt). Many people are happy just to get rid of things, but it is *always* wise to ask.

Collect wild protected materials

In this uber-connected world, it's very possible to find what you are looking for completely legally by searching out a legitimate source. Know the laws of the land; there's nothing more embarrassing (and perhaps more costly) than having a park ranger go through the contents of your bluebell-stuffed backpack while your three-year-old is watching.

Resource: Plants

All the hardscaping and tchotchkes aside, if you don't have plants, it's hard to have a garden. Thankfully, there are many ways you can acquire plants without spending a lot of money:

Seed starting

Starting your own plants from seed is one of the cheapest ways of getting what you want when you want it, particularly when it comes to annual vegetables and flowers. If you've let the big companies convince you that it's easier to just "let them do the hard work," you are selling yourself short. Anyone can grow their own plants from seed, and in Chapter 8 I'll discuss a wonderful way of doing so without having to bring the dirt inside.

Striking cuttings

The very first time I rooted a cutting was completely by accident. I'd cut a huge bunch of colorful coleus stems for a vase and put them on my table. Two weeks later roots were growing from each stem, and I felt like a genius.

I've rooted a great deal of cuttings since then (and rotted a few too), but the wonderful thing about propagating plants yourself is the great sense of accomplishment—and the knowledge that the process is free. Some may take, some may not, but you will be growing your skill base as well as your plant collection in the process. In Chapter 8 I'll help make this process even easier by introducing you to the Forsythe pot—my very favorite way of rooting new plants.

Divisions from others

Gardeners are generous people. When we see others taking an interest in this mildly obsessive pursuit—and

Boxwood roots very easily and can save you a lot of money on sophisticated edgings.

proving themselves to be more than just fair-weather gardeners—we fall all over ourselves to help them. That includes giving them plants . . . lots of them. It's only when you start competing with us over a variegated clivia cultivar or hard-to-find yucca that we can get a little testy.

Until then, we've got buckets of daisies and coneflowers and daylilies and iris and hosta to throw at you if you'll take them.

Buy one bugleweed and you'll be able to make ten for yourself and share another five.

How do you find us? If you're not part of a local gardening group, then look around your neighborhood and search out some of the best gardens. In early spring or early fall, knock on the door or, if you're shy, leave a note on the step introducing yourself and letting them know that you would be very happy for any surplus they may have. Speaking for myself, I would read such a note with tears in my eyes and put your number on speed dial. Gardeners HATE to throw away plants.

Local plant sales

Look for sales sponsored by the local high school and college horticulture classes, which sell plants (usually cheaply) in order to support their programs. Other plant sales in your community might be sponsored by the county Master Gardener program, a local garden club, or public garden. By going to these sales you can not only find slightly cheaper plants, but you can also meet new gardeners in your area. Start by contacting your local high school or county Master Gardeners.

Plant swaps

This is where the fun happens. In order to talk about all things green without putting everyone around you to sleep, you should be thinking about joining a garden club or organization. One of the biggest bonuses of doing so (besides the stimulating conversation) is attending a plant swap with gardeners who are even more obsessed than you are. This means plants. Good plants. And most swaps allow you to come empty-handed at first (though you might have to wait until those rare yuccas are all gone before you can start grabbing).

Death racks

It's hard to pick up a half-dead plant on a clearance rack and imagine it vibrant and lush, but doing so, particularly with perennials and shrubs, is an excellent way of saving huge

Fall clearance racks only save you money if you know where you're going to plant all those three-dollar specials before winter comes.

amounts of money in the garden and being able to afford plants you might otherwise have to skip. Next time you're in a big box nursery center, do yourself a favor and spend a little time loitering in the very back of the store, where they no longer make any attempt to keep things attractive. Have your phone ready so you can look up unknown plants. Pull them out of their pots to check if they're terribly root bound; if they are, let someone else take a chance on them. Likewise, never buy a clearance plant with obvious signs of disease or pests.

Keep your garden plan in mind. You're not saving money if you're buying plants you don't need just because they're cheap. When you come home with the forty-six plants you "rescued" for twenty dollars, give them a good soaking in a tub, cut them back if needed, and then get them in the ground . . . fast. If they're pushing the limits of your zone and it's autumn, then cover the pots in mulch to overwinter without root shock.

Resource: Hardscape Materials

Finding hardscape materials is a question of opening your eyes, always being ready to spring into action, and never being afraid to ask. Keeping a pair of gloves in the car is also a good idea.

Reclaimed brick beautifully doubled the height of this garden wall.

Big Dreams, Small Garden

How'd I get my "thousands of antique bricks?" I was walking with my children in our neighborhood and was surprised to see the city tearing up the one hundred-year-old dry-laid brick sidewalks. Though I was annoyed at the loss to the city's history, I saw an opportunity and asked the men taking up the bricks where they were going. They put me in touch with their supervisor who told me that if I was willing to dig them out of a dirt pile, I was welcome to them.

That summer (with a three-year-old and a six-year-old "helping") I transferred twenty-five hundred bricks destined for the dump to my burgeoning garden. An added bonus was that most of the bricks had been made 100 years before in a brickyard not a quarter mile from my home.

I have since added to these bricks with small piles either leftover from friends' finished building projects or abandoned building projects in my community. I always ask, and most of the time I receive. Don't be afraid to do the same with:

Lumber—When people finish a deck, fence, or shed, they often have no place to store the extra lumber and are happy to get rid of it as quickly as possible (especially if they live in a subdivision with strict rules about such things). Decking rails make excellent trellising materials, and you never know when a four-by-four post is going to come in handy.

Stone—Excavation = Opportunity. Watching my old neighborhood carved up by tiny spec houses was very difficult. The only thing that made it bearable was the fact that the developer allowed me to take away all the stone I could carry from the building sites. He probably didn't think I could carry that much, but righteous anger is a great motivator. Pretty soon I had low stone walls and flagstone pathways, and the privet hedge had grown up sufficiently enough to mask the changing view—the "price" I had paid for my hardscape materials.

Large moving equipment in your general vicinity should always make you clear your throat and utter the words, "May I?" Sometimes the stones are needed as backfill, but often there are more than enough to share.

Think creatively. Sometimes hardscaping materials are as close as your own kitchen.

Mulch/compost—Before I start advising you to harangue the tree trimmers in your neighborhood, one of the best ways of getting free or reduced-price mulch and compost is to find out if your county landfill has it. Some counties even load the mulch right into your trailer. In my county in Maryland, I could fill my nine-by-thirteen-by-two-foot trailer (or friend's truck) with good double-shred mulch or stringently tested compost for ten dollars. What a deal!

As for those wonderful tree trimmers who keep our roadways and electric lines clear, they often need a place close by to dump their chippings, and it's worth stopping and asking. It's green stuff at first, suitable for pathways and play areas, but after a season or two it breaks down wonderfully and can be used for garden beds.

Soil—If you're in need of fill dirt, contact the landscaping companies in your area by phone or email and let them know they can dump excavated dirt. You will not be getting the good stuff, but if you need to fill in a low spot, level a lawn, or need dirt to mix with good compost to create good soil, landscaping companies digging pools and ponds will most likely be happy to have somewhere to dump it.

Resource: Recycled materials

It's remarkable how much Americans throw away—and how rampant consumerism has quietly shaped our thinking when it comes to objects that we need or desire . . . and then need or desire again. Each time I come across a weed whacker at a yard sale that just needs a new string cartridge, or a pair of good pruners that only need sharpening and a bit of WD-40, I am at once elated and disheartened. Elated that I've made out like a bandit, disheartened because the tendency to throw things away and replace them is quickly filling our landfills and emptying our bank accounts.

However much this trend may disturb me, there is no doubt that I have spent much of my life capitalizing on what others are willing to get rid of—and my garden is a testament to that lifestyle.

Recycled materials can be used in the way in which they were intended—by refurbishing a string trimmer for instance, or spray painting a patio table—or you can get creative and use a brightly painted wooden ladder

This wheelbarrow was dragged out from behind a city apartment complex where it had been discarded. It has been home to lettuce and cabbage and now more permanently functions as a succulent planter.

as a bit of folk art in the middle of your tomatoes, or use a chair frame to hold up a huge stand of flopping daisies.

When you're trying to save money, you've got to do the footwork, keeping your eyes peeled for side-of-the-road freebies and thrift/junk stores off the beaten path. Don't make the mistake of going to faux-rustic country sales to purchase a repurposed item for a repurposed price. Make your own magic in the garden.

The best part about using recycled materials is that there is no wrong way to use them. Today's quirky uses are tomorrow's trends: witness the innovative way that gardeners have been repurposing pallets over the last five years.

We don't have to buy new. Sometimes we don't even have to buy old. Using the cast-offs from a disposable culture is not only a brilliant way of equipping and accessorizing our gardens, it's a small way of opting out of the consumerist mentality and helping our environment in the process.

This spray painted seat-less chair makes a fantastic staking mechanism for the ornamental grass that will grow through it during the season.

Wire hangers make great garden staples.

A WHIMSICAL GARDEN

" I'm a bottom-feeder waiting for the stuff that settles," says Jan Faulkner with a hearty laugh that shakes her slight but muscular frame. However, those who are lucky enough to visit her tucked-away city garden see anything but trash.

Instead, whimsical, colorful collections of plants, containers, and unexpected objects are expertly

arranged around pathways that lead the visitor through garden rooms and sitting areas. All aspects of the garden frame her gorgeous bungalow—painted a rich mustard yellow with soft green trim, it reminds one of exclusive Northern California beach communities, not a small Maryland city next to the train tracks.

Jan has been gardening her property for twenty-eight years, ever since moving in as a single mother with two small girls. Where others saw a tiny bungalow on a marginal sloped lot right on a busy, blind corner, Jan saw garden potential. But she is quick to point out that she had very limited choices on her budget.

That budget hasn't changed much in two decades, but her garden surely has. "It's important to put your initial energy into your daily pathways first," she advises. "Your emotional needs for the garden are met and reinforced this way."

A yoga instructor, private gardener, and proprietor of a tropical plant business that caters to large city buildings, Jan has plenty of experience with far wealthier gardeners who struggle with contentment issues even though designers, materials, and paid help are at their fingertips. "You've got to get rid of the ego," says Jan in true yoga fashion, sitting comfortably on her bohemian porch furnished entirely from thrift store and side-of-the-road finds, adding thoughtfully, "Beauty is in the use of something."

Her garden could not illustrate this sentiment any better. A cast-off watering trough in the vegetable garden is painted lime green and houses

salad greens and chard. An industrial shelving unit sits waiting for a coat of paint and no doubt many colorful pots. Jan has a frugal spirit and a collector's heart, but unlike many collectors, she regularly holds informal yard sales—charging very little for some of her most precious finds.

"I like to use something for a while, and then send it back out into the universe," she explains. "It keeps my space from becoming too cluttered and allows me the opportunity to experience the beauty of an object for a short time."

Her deep sense of contentment is palpable and at once calming. And the inspirational garden that she has created with limited time and money has become a haven for her family, friends, pets . . . and herself.

7

MANAGING YOUR GARDEN PROJECTS

"Experience is the teacher of all things."
—Julius Caesar

You might not think of the creation of your garden as a project that *needs* a manager. In fact, the idea of treating it this way might put you off the whole process entirely. Yet, consider these eight factors that *will* affect your garden and have "project management" written all over them.

- Goals—You've got them.
- Budget—You'll need one.
- Time—You don't have much.
- Obstacles—You've identified them.
- Materials—Cheap is good, free is better.
- Resources—From nurseries to plant swaps.
- Monitoring—Is what you're doing working?
- Record Keeping—There's only so much you can remember.

It's been my experience that viewing the garden as a series of mini projects within a greater project and plan allows the gardener to take advantage of opportunities, manage limited resources and time effectively, and provides a sense of accomplishment as projects are completed.

Some projects are going to take more in the way of time and resources. Approaching these mindfully will save you both.

Hey, I'm a gardener, not a project manager!

If the above sounds way too complicated, just think of it as working smart. It's taking a realistic goal, carefully setting out the steps needed, and implementing them.

Let's see it in action:

Jane Gardener has a lot planned for her plain urban lot sandwiched between other plain urban lots, such as patio seating, a flower garden, and a small koi pond. But above all else, she wants a twenty-by-thirty-foot vegetable garden this year. She knows that deer grazing will be an issue and that her soil is compacted and poor. She doesn't have money for a fence, but might be able to save for one for next year, so she'll need to save money where she can toward that goal. What should she do?

a) Forget about gardening until next year.
    Well that's depressing, especially if funds are short next year too.

b) Get fired up in the spring, cultivate a twenty-by-thirty-foot patch, amend it with bagged compost and manure, buy a bunch of vegetable seedlings at the nursery, plant her seedlings, ignore the deer, and hope for the best.
    Oh boy. A time and money sink and doomed to failure. Have you ever heard "ignore the deer" and "hope for the best" paired successfully in a sentence?

c) Get fired up in the spring, rack up four thousand dollars' worth of credit card debt for a contractor to put in a fence around her entire lot, then amend the soil as above and plant her nursery plants.
    Yikes! Expensive, risky, and scary. Tomatoes are meant to lift mortgages, not add to them.

d) Put her project manager hat on and work smart, allowing her to improve the soil, grow vegetables, thwart deer, all whilst working toward next year's goals.
    Well, the answer is obviously "d" (quiz answers usually are). Here's why:

In late winter (giving herself plenty of **time**), Jane revisits her **budget** and her **goals** for planting. She decides to use temporary, less expensive fencing that will protect a smaller ten-by-ten-foot section of plants against the huge **obstacle** of grazing deer. Those **materials** can then be used elsewhere in the garden when the real fence goes

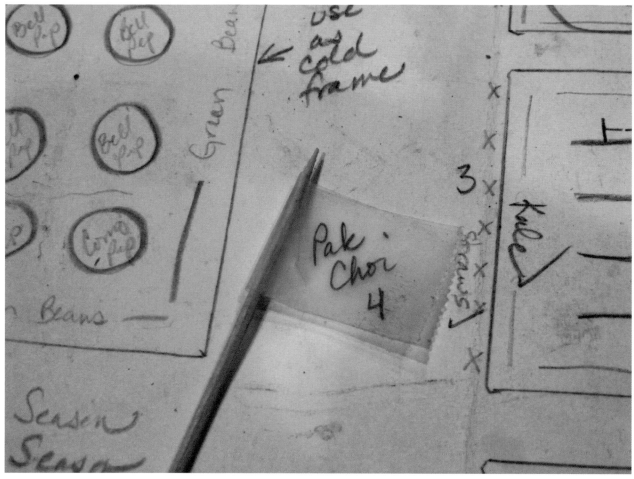

Don't grow more seedlings than you need. A project plan helps you see what you actually have room for.

in. A smaller amount of growing space means she can use the space above her fridge to raise enough seedlings with one grow light.

Meanwhile, she'll put her efforts into researching and obtaining sufficient bulk amendments from **resources** such as the county landfill and neighboring farms to start smothering the turf and building the soil for the eventual twenty-by-thirty-foot vegetable garden.

Halfway through the season she comes across a beautiful second-hand table and chairs. Knowing that she'll be working on that project next spring, she buys them and sets them up where she thinks she'll be putting in a patio, allowing her to **monitor** placement and decide if that's the right site before she invests in paving materials.

Next year she can tackle the fence if funds are available, or use those funds to build her patio and keep a smaller vegetable garden, which, thanks to her **record**

keeping, turns out to be all the produce she can actually handle. The soil she amended will instead be used for a flower and herb garden, where she'll grow highly deer-resistant plants, such as daffodils, iris, lavender, and rosemary, which she obtained and planted during the autumn plant exchanges and sales.

Option "d" sees her tackling the problem thoughtfully, within her budget, and with a view to further implementation of the overall project next year. It's working smart. It's project management, and I bet she didn't even know it.

The dreaded B word

A budget, by its very definition, is a limitation, and the single most influential factor in achieving your goals. If funds were no object, Jane Gardener, you, me, and the rest of the ninety-niners wouldn't need to be such careful project managers. Jane could install a seven-foot-high fence, put a patio in, rip it out, put it somewhere better, and then just move somewhere else with a huge deck and a neighboring farmers' market.

If you want to eventually build a deck, budgeting carefully can make that goal a reality. Without a big income change, it just won't happen on its own.

But funds *are* an object. In fact, they're very objectionable indeed. And whether we're willing to admit to and set an actual budget for the garden or not, the availability of funds will drive what we are able to achieve and when. Personally, I'd rather have a good idea of what those funds are, rather than robbing Peter to pay Paul and always coming up short.

If you're smart, you already have a household budget that you stick to. Look at it carefully and decide if you can subtract a certain amount of money each month to spend on current garden projects and to save for future garden projects.

It may be a very small amount indeed. That's okay—just identify *what* it is so you can move forward.

Projects within the greater project

Now, time to stop focusing on the big picture and look at the small ones. When you think of your garden as a series of little projects within the ultimate goal of an attractive and functional space, you can prioritize those projects, set individual budgets, and identify the materials you will need to complete each job. Though your budget is the most important factor, your next priority is timing. Which project makes the most sense to accomplish first? And which projects rely on the completion of another?

For instance, John and Julie, our suburban couple in Chapter 4, wanted fruit trees in their garden and a lawn for their children. They also wanted to screen nosy neighbors, plant vegetable and flower gardens, build a patio, and have some sort of water feature.

- If they wait to plant the fruit trees until they've put in everything else, they will have lost years of having fresh apples from their own trees. The trees are relatively inexpensive and priority should be given to planting them right away.
- If they wait to screen the neighbors and start the patio first, they will have lost years of growth on a hedge and will be forced to look at the junk under the neighbor's deck while they're eating al fresco pasta. If this screen is important to them, it should be planted before they build the patio.

Disguising a chain-link fence can be done with hedging or the clever use of bamboo screening.

Plants take time to grow. If you have well-defined design goals already (i.e., a hedge here, a fruit tree there), it is wise to put your resources toward these anchor items, categorizing them in terms of high, medium, and low priorities.

And, if you have a hard time keeping all this straight at any one time, I have a solution for you.

The simplicity of project sheets

Because I *am* a gardener, and not a professional project manager, I don't need to mess with flow charts, process models, Gantt charts, or time cards. I can manage my garden projects any way I like to, and the way that works best for me is by creating a simple project sheet for each individual goal I have set during the planning phase. This keeps me aware of my budget and priorities.

The project sheet is devoted to *one goal only*. This keeps it clear and focused—keeping *me* clear and focused.

After I have identified my goal and figured out how I am going to implement it, I fill in the sheet and put it in my journal. This keeps me organized, on track, and when I forget what I am supposed to be working on next, I have an instant reminder of my priorities.

Here's an example using our couple:

John and Julie want a screen from difficult neighbors on the north side of their house. This is a high-priority project, so they're willing to spend a little money. However, they cannot afford a fence, and the area is lightly shaded by the house.

After researching options, they decide that Manhattan euonymus will work well as an evergreen screen as it tolerates shade, is a fast grower, can be trimmed, and one-gallon pots are exceedingly cheap (as evergreen hedges go). It also layers well, so they have the option of propagating more plants in the future if needed.

Here's their project sheet:

Project Sheet I

Goal: Evergreen Screen on Northwest Boundary	
Budget:	$110
Priority:	High
Timing:	March/April current year
Materials needed:	12 Manhattan euonymus in 1-gallon pots Bulk compost
Resource:	Big box nursery center—cheapest plants County landfill
Notes:	Planting on 4-foot centers Check property boundary with neighbor
Completed:	
Actual Cost:	$

If between now and March they suddenly become bosom friends with their neighbors (who have miraculously turned over a new leaf and decided to fill their entire garden with flowers instead of old cars), they can remove this project (and sheet) from the overall list and use the funds for the next high-priority project they have outlined in their journal.

But it's not just the high-priority projects that need an outline. Knowing what your low-priority projects will cost you and what you'll need for them is just as important. That way you can implement them if priorities or resources change. Here's a sheet for John and Julie's lowest priority:

Project Sheet II

Goal: Container Water Feature	
Budget:	$150
Priority:	Low
Timing:	After patio is completed As funds are available If container is found cheaply
Materials needed:	Large ceramic container without hole Small pump 3–5 aquatic plants
Resource:	Local specialty nursery Yard sales Big box nursery center
Notes:	Pump (>120 gph) Plant considerations: colocasia, papyrus, water hyacinth, water lettuce, canna lily
Completed:	✓ Fall 2017
Actual Cost:	✓ $50 (container $15 plants $15 pump $20)

The cost for this project was high relative to the need for it, consequently it was judged to be a low priority. However, midseason, Julie came across a perfect container for a medium-sized water feature at a yard sale. She paid fifteen dollars for it, which was one hundred and five dollars less than she'd thought she'd pay at a ceramics retailer. Since they had the container, they went ahead with the project, paying fifteen dollars for three plants and getting

All projects look worse before they look better.

divisions of two others from a friend with a pond. The last cost was a pump and hose, which cost twenty dollars. Total spent: fifty bucks.

One of the best things about project sheets is watching yourself achieve a stated goal. That feels fantastic when you've got a lot of work ahead of you.

Use digital photographs to document the stages of each project—and for heaven's sake, take the time to print them out and add them to your project sheets before they're lost in an unfortunate incident with an overheated hard drive. You never know when you'd like to show a fellow gardener how a space has evolved over time, or when a newbie gardener is going to visit your mature garden and ask, "How'd it look before?"

Try using project sheets yourself; you can find a blank one in the appendices at the end of the book to photocopy for your own use.

A manager needs an office

A work area does not have to be perfect. For much of our early married years, our rental flat was too small for a desk, much less an office. I used to keep my laptop, a stapler, a couple

Even centrally located potting stations can be slightly hidden away with plantings.

pens, a notepad, and paperclips in a cardboard box that I could bring to the dining room table when needed, and then put away under my bed when it was time to shovel food into children. That box was my portable work station. It kept me organized, kept oatmeal off the bills, and I felt less chaotic.

No matter how small your garden space, you need a work station. A work station is where you pot up plants, keep tools and materials, maybe even baby a plant or two. If you're lucky enough to have a yard, you should carve out a small part of it for this area. If you only have a patio or a balcony, you can still do it, but you might want to make it attractive as well as functional, maybe using an old dresser or table.

Claiming this space is, in effect, claiming your office. Beats a cube any day of the week.

A RENTED URBAN FARM

What happens when three generations of your family have lived, loved, and gardened in a neighborhood that is no longer affordable enough for you to do the same? For Sheila Cassani and Matthew Yungert, natives of one of the highest priced metro areas in the nation, Oakland, California, the answer is to rent.

But Sheila and Matthew don't treat their one-bedroom rented home as a temporary stopping point. Artichokes spring from rustically edged vegetable beds, apple trees are laden with fruit, and in a temperate Mediterranean climate, kale and collards provide fresh greens all year long. Add a beehive and six chickens, and you've got the makings of an urban homestead lovingly named Kansas Street Farm, a rented urban homestead.

The multi-unit property consists of a large house with attached studio flat and their little cottage in the back. Sheila and Matthew have lived there since 2006 with one short break while they were studying abroad.

Now, the rented units are surrounded by overflowing, productive gardens that provide fruit, vegetables, habitat for pollinators, and a riot of color. I ask Sheila what their landlord think of the property's metamorphosis and how the young couple went about asking them for permission.

"Our approach was to ask forgiveness," she says with a chuckle. "But once they saw how dedicated we were and how much our landscaping was helping their property values, they were happy about it. A little surprised maybe, but happy."

Because they are renting, the couple used available materials from the property first, creating edging with old bricks and bits of concrete, revitalizing an old apple tree and reclaiming an old raised bed. When they need something now they search Craigslist and Freecycle first, always keeping their financial investment small. High-value plants, such as figs, avocados, and kaffir limes, are planted in portable containers.

"We love free," says Sheila, an anthropology major who now works with a community organization that gives grants to small farms nationwide. Matthew is a project manager with an architectural concrete firm and enjoys creating quirky, functional furniture from castoffs like pallets and old beams. Even their curtain rods are made from bamboo they harvested off the property.

I ask Sheila, "Is it frustrating to not be able to buy a home and create more of this?" She doesn't hesitate in answering, "Absolutely."

They both are college educated—and have the loans to show for it. Both have well-paying jobs, but in this older mixed-income, middle-class neighborhood, where most houses are instantly snapped up with cash offers, homes are out of reach.

"But there's a feeling of sanctuary here," Sheila says. "For us, for our friends. We don't know how long we'll be here, but while we're here, this place is our home." And, soon it will be home to three, as Matthew and Sheila are expecting their first baby.

Their advice to others in similar situations is simple, but powerful. "Experiment. Stay open-minded. You don't have to be an expert when you find joy in something."

There is certainly joy at Kansas Street Farm. Joy and passion fruit and six hens with personality. Home sweet home indeed.

8

BUILDING SKILLS

*"Training is everything. The peach was once a bitter almond;
cauliflower is nothing but cabbage with a college education."*
—Mark Twain

We all have jobs we're better at than others. Natural ability plays a big role here, but so does our *desire* to learn. In turn, that desire is based on two things, a) natural love of a subject, and b) necessity.

For instance, interested in small motors, I've fixed my heavy-duty mixer twice, but feel exasperated when the sink starts leaking, because I hate plumbing. YouTube taught me how to fix the mixer; it could certainly teach me how to fix the sink. I just happen to know that my husband will eventually do it.

The better we want our gardens to look (and the less money we have to hire craftsmen or pay for plants), the more we must create, fix, and build for ourselves. Our efforts will not be perfect the first time, nor the second, but as we get more comfortable with these skills, we'll find that we look forward to challenging ourselves with something else.

First, we must *choose to try*. I don't have an innate talent for woodworking, but after forcing myself to figure it out, I can construct a very basic cold frame or gate arbor. Believe me, the sense of accomplishment when you can say "I built/created/grew that myself" is worth the study time and inevitable mistakes.

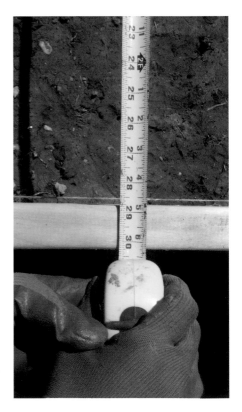

Don't be afraid to build new skills.

Some skills will save you more money than others, and others will amortize over a longer period. For instance, buying all the pieces to make a rain barrel is usually more expensive than buying a prebuilt one from a city municipality that is trying to encourage citizens to save water. Seed starting may occasion a small initial investment of lights, trays, and seeds, but depending on how many plants you grow in the following years, and how many recycled materials you use, it could save you hundreds.

There are so many skills I could discuss here, however, I'm going to focus on four that I feel should be part of any gardener's skill set:

- Seed starting
- Propagation by cuttings
- Building raised beds and cold frames
- Pruning

It is beyond the scope of this book to cover everything about skills that have entire books written about them individually, so each section ends with recommendations to provide further in-depth references for gardeners who are determined to build their knowledge base.

Seed starting

When you start your own seeds you can choose the specific varieties you wish to grow, save money on large quantities of plants, and provide seedlings to swap with others. It can be a simple process or a complex one, but the majority of common garden seeds sprout with just a bit of soil, light, water, and heat. Starting plants from seed is grouped into two divisions: direct and indirect planting.

When you're tired of shoveling snow, sorting through your seeds for the season ahead provides a bit of hope.

Direct planting is putting seeds straight into the ground at the right time of year to germinate and grow precisely where you put them. Root vegetables, such as beets and carrots, lettuces and other greens, and many other vegetables grow well this way, particularly if you do not suffer from pests such as slugs and flocks of early morning starlings looking for a salad.

In addition to these, I like to direct sow many of my annual and biennial flowers, such as larkspur, verbascum, nigella, lunaria, poppies, cosmos, and zinnia, especially since I usually get away with haphazardly scattering them in the garden at the time of year when they would normally seed themselves.

Indirect planting refers to the process of sowing seeds in flats, germinating them, pricking them out, transplanting them, hardening them off, and eventually planting them. If that sounds horrendously complicated, let me introduce you to a method used by thousands of gardeners over the last few years that relies on recycled containers to create mini green-houses outdoors.

This method allows you to sow seeds any time from fall to late winter, which will then germinate when conditions are right for them to do so. Consequently, you get seedlings sooner than you would if you planted directly outdoors, but later than those you might start inside under lights. The trade-off in hassle factor is usually worth it

Happy seedlings poke out from an improvised milk jug greenhouse.

Building Skills

You can modify most lidded plastic containers when you use this method, but like many gardeners, I like to use milk jugs due to their availability, height, perfectly sized air vent and convenient handle. I sow seeds both inside and out, but there is no doubt that using this method means less inside mess, less timing worries, and lots of happy, well-adjusted seedlings.

I like to increase my chances of success still further by sowing in late January or early February—potentially offsetting losses from seeds rotting over the winter.

Materials:
- Opaque gallon milk jugs or water jugs, rinsed well
- Duct tape
- Seed starting mix
- Seeds—start with something easy, like tomatoes or lettuce

Tools:
- Scissors
- Small knife
- Sharpie marker

Directions:
- Starting just to the right and under the bottom of the handle of a milk jug, cut the jug in half, crosswise, ending on the other side of the handle so you create a hinge.
- Pull the top back and use the knife to punch five drainage holes in the bottom.
- Fill the bottom with seed starting mix.
- Plant your seeds as directed on the packet, remembering that each seed will potentially need

Milk jugs are filled with soil and ready for seeds and labeling.

to be transplanted and hardened off, so don't go crazy.
- Due to differences in germination and size, don't mix your seeds (with the exception of different varieties of the same plant).
- Close up the jug and tape it closed. *Do not put the lid back on the top—ventilation is crucial.*

Big Dreams, Small Garden

- Label your jugs clearly with a marker. Place them in a south-facing location outside and watch for signs of germination. Once they have germinated, be sure to give them adequate moisture.
- Once seedlings are sporting their first true leaves, they will need to be transplanted into their own small pots. Don't push this step too long or you'll end up with leggy seedlings competing against too many of their siblings.
- Prick them out with a fork and replant into two- or three-inch pots filled with good-quality potting soil.

Once seeds are planted in the jugs, duct tape them closed and clearly label them, leaving the lid off.

Some of your cool-weather seedlings may be ready to go straight into the garden, but many will need additional protection in a cold frame or in a basement under lights until the weather starts to change, allowing you to get them used to the outdoors and fluctuating temperatures that can be tough on tender seedlings.

When seedlings are big enough, prick them out and put them into individual pots or flats.

Seedlings raised this way tend to be a bit hardier anyway, so a cold frame or a rack covered in plastic usually works just fine; slowly open the plastic during the day, then close it at night to harden them off.

I recommend:

My two favorite texts on seed starting are the comprehensive *Growing Herbs and Vegetables* by Terry and Mark Silber and the wonderfully witty *Garden Flowers from Seed* by Christopher Lloyd and Graham Rice.

Basic propagation from herbaceous or softwood cuttings

There are many ways of propagating plants asexually. One of the very easiest and cheapest is to simply take pencil-size cuttings of favored shrubs in the autumn and push them into good soft soil to overwinter. No fuss, no bother. About half of them will start growing their own roots by mid-spring. It doesn't cost any money and takes just a little time.

If you want slightly better odds of success, let me introduce you to something called the Forsythe pot technique. It's not much more complicated and can be a lot of fun, inspiring you to propagate more plants each time you empty this little factory of its rooted cuttings.

A quick note, however: plants do not uniformly offer up their cuttings at the same time; one has to pay attention to specific schedules and growth patterns for the plant and take soft (pliable) or hardwood (woody) shoots accordingly—I offer a book suggestion at the end of this section to help guide you with the what and when.

As for the how? That's easy. The Forsythe pot is a pot within a pot that keeps cuttings in a perfect environment for maximum success. Here's how to make one.

A pocketful of cuttings can become a garden full of new plants.

Cuttings sit comfortably in a Forsythe pot: A ring of vermiculite constantly moistened by a reservoir of water.

Materials:
- 10- to 12-inch-diameter plastic or glazed ceramic pot with or without drainage holes.
- 3- to 4-inch unglazed terracotta pot without drainage holes.
- Small bag of horticultural vermiculite (available at garden centers).
- Jar of fresh, powdered rooting hormone (available at garden centers).

Directions:

- Make sure any large drainage holes are somewhat blocked with gravel or pot shards, then fill the larger pot with vermiculite to within 2 inches of the top.
- Nestle the second smaller pot into the middle of the vermiculite so that the top of the pot is not more than a half inch from the top of the vermiculite.
- Fill the second pot with water and lightly moisten the vermiculite.
- Make a three-inch cutting from the tip of your parent plant, cutting just below a node or leaf axil. Remove the bottom leaves from your cutting and moisten the bottom by lightly dipping it in rooting hormone. Use a pencil to make a small hole in the vermiculite ring between the two pots, then firm the cutting in. For extra humidity I cover the entire thing in a transparent plastic bag.

Remove all but the top leaves on your softwood cutting.

Over the course of a day or two, the water will slowly seep from the walls of the inner pot, keeping the vermiculite at a constant state of ideal dampness, perfect for getting those cuttings off the ground and rooted. Once the cuttings have put out a fragile system of roots, they can be potted up and hardened off outdoors. Make sure to keep the pot topped up with water. Some of your cuttings will not take, but that's okay; it's a cheap experiment and is helped with more study.

Without a greenhouse, the Forsythe pot literally revolutionized my propagation

Hardwood cuttings of boxwood overwinter in a tented Forsythe pot near aloes and succulents.

efforts. I still start hundreds of seeds in the spring, water-root coleus and willow, and divide perennials until my hands ache, but now when I am in a friend's garden and I see something I really want, I know that I've got a propagator ready to take the cutting.

I recommend:

Secrets of Plant Propagation by Lewis Hill is a terrific manual that will expand your knowledge base without bogging you down with minutiae. It was voted as one of America's 75 best garden books by the American Horticultural Society, and for good reason.

Building raised beds and cold frames

Cold frames will extend your season or protect precious plants.

You may not use raised beds in your garden, but having a cold frame in order to over-winter precious plants, harden-off seedlings, or eat lettuce in December is worth learning how to use a saw and a drill, and a very basic cold frame is just a raised bed with a glass or heavy plastic cover.

If you wish to build a cold frame from the beginning, it is wise to procure glass (old window, door, etc.) first, and then build a frame to fit, rather than building the traditional four-by-eight-foot bed outlined below.

Materials:

- Twenty-four linear feet of two-by-twelve lumber (two eight-foot sections and two four-foot sections). Treated vs. untreated lumber is always a hot topic, but in recent years the chemicals used have not been as caustic for the environment, your plants, and you. I use scrap lumber (whatever I can get), but when I use treated, the beds last longer.
- Twelve three-inch wood screws.

You can save a lot of money by buying half-price scrap lumber from lumberyards.

Tools:

- Handheld cordless drill/driver. A good-quality cordless drill/driver is one of the best investments you can make. You will use it time and time again inside and out. If you don't have one, borrow one from a friend.
- Drill bit with a slightly smaller diameter than your screws.
- Either an electric rotary saw or a handheld wood saw.
- Pencil and ruler for marking.
- Builder's level (borrow one!).

Directions:

- Cut the wood into two eight-foot-long sections and two four-foot-long sections.
- On a flat surface, position three of the boards so they create a U shape, with one of the four-foot sections between the two eight-foot sections. If the wood shows a strongly curved grain on the edge, position it so it curves into the bed, not against it.

Having another person helping makes a difference, as does stacking beds on top of one another for a flat working surface.

- You'll need someone to hold the boards while you predrill three two-inch-deep holes for the connecting screws in the top, middle, and bottom ends of each eight-foot section leading into the ends of the four-foot sections. Make sure the tops of your boards line up exactly.
- Screw the wood screws into the holes you've just drilled.
- Add the second four-foot piece of wood and drill/screw it into place.

- Position the raised bed on a flat surface to prevent warping—you'll need another person to help you. Use bricks or rocks as shims under corners where needed to ensure that you have a level surface.
- Fill your bed with a mixture of half compost and half native soil and buy a small soil test kit to see if you'll need to add any further amendments. You're now ready to start growing!

If you're using your raised bed as a basic cold frame, simply leave out the dirt and put an old storm door or storm window(s) over the frame.

If you wish to make a traditional sloped cold frame to take advantage of all available sunlight and shed water easily, add another piece of two-by-twelve to the back and sides and cut the two sides at a diagonal toward the front. You'll need to use braces to hold the original box to the sloped box, but these can be as easy as pieces of a one-by-two screwed into both. Old hinges fastened to the back of the frame and the windows will make it much easier to access.

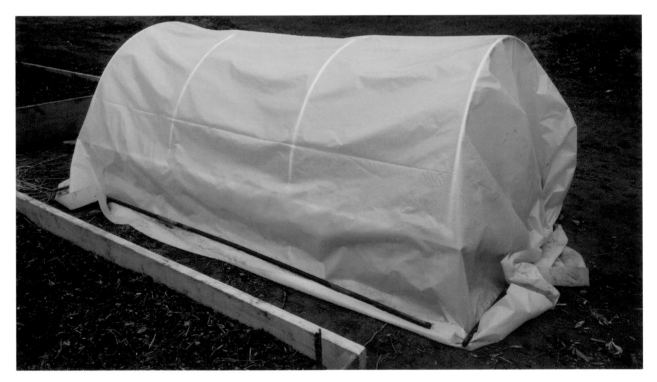

Using CPVC hoops and six-mil plastic converts a raised bed into a mini greenhouse.

I recommend:
Mel Bartholemew's *All New Square Foot Gardening* can help you make the most out of your raised bed. Eliot Coleman's inspiring *Four-Season Harvest* will get you using your cold frame . . . and maybe thinking about hoop and greenhouses, too!

Pruning

Many gardeners are surprisingly frightened of pruning their plants and, consequently, don't act until it's pretty late in the game when they are then forced to do a hard pruning into ancient wood. Some plants will be forgiving, but others, such as juniper or lavender, won't be, so don't wait.

Much of pruning is common sense, and 80 percent of the time you're not going to kill the plant if you mess up. You may impact that season's flowering/fruiting or end up a little challenged in the aesthetics department, but eventually it should grow back. This is how we learn.

Smart pruning makes for healthier plants.

Instead of approaching pruning as a multi-stepped project, read through the guidelines below and apply them to the plant you are facing at high noon. Don't be afraid. With the exception of rose bushes, you're the only one who's armed.

Preventative measures

Wherever possible, try not to create a problem in the first place. Don't plant a fifty-foot arborvitae in front of a window just because it's a lovely four-foot pyramid right now. Don't buy a standard rootstock apple tree if you have no plans to buy a corresponding ladder. Research your plant choice. If you love to shape and prune plants, then you can bend the rules a bit, but buying the right-sized plant for the space is the best way to start.

Timing

Most woody plants and trees are best dealt with during their dormant season, however, if they are early spring bloomers, like forsythia or quince, prune them as soon as the flowers have faded and new growth begins.

Cutting summer blooming perennials down in late spring to promote bushier, more manageable plants is a great move for notorious floppers. These mums will get a pixie cut at the end of May.

There are exceptions to this rule, of course. For instance, I like to trim my boxwood late in the summer after new growth has established to keep them neat and less stressed. A pruning guide helps out tremendously for knowing when to prune.

Perennials can be cut back as soon as they have finished flowering (sometimes to encourage a second flush). However, if you wish to leave seed heads for the birds, then cut them back in late winter.

The right tool for the job

Buy good tools. Your first purchase should be a pair of good bypass pruners that feel good in your hand and have steel blades that are able to hold an edge. Next, a pair of long-handled loppers, again with a good blade that can handle branches up to an inch and a half in diameter. Paint the handles of both a bright orange or red so it's harder to lose them, then invest in a small handheld sharpener to hone the blades and keep them cutting true.

Your next tool should be a handheld pruning saw to take care of anything bigger. These have serrated blades, and the best ones fold up for easy storage. A pair of shears will make hedge trimming a lot easier, as will a telescoping pole pruner when you've got a twenty-foot rambling rose growing up a trellis. Most gardeners acquire more specialized tools slowly, as they are needed.

A folding pruning saw takes care of branches that are too large for loppers.

Don't make a mess of it

Be clean in your cuts. When you crush a branch or leave ragged edges, you open the door to disease and insects. Sometimes you can even spread fatal diseases between plants. Keep your tools sharp, and if a branch is too big, stop what you're doing and move up to the next size tool.

Keep stepping back

Make a cut or two, then step back and look at the overall shape and what you are accomplishing. Never assume you've chosen the right branch until you've stepped back and made sure.

Don't create brooms

Pruning a plant will encourage new growth from the node(s) below your cut. Some shrubs can react with a broom effect, where the tip of your branch sprouts several new shoots and looks terrible. Instead, cut farther down or even at the base to make the plant bushier from within.

Making the cut

- Cut out all dead or diseased wood.
- If you can see buds or nodes, cut just above them by about a quarter inch at a slant away from the bud on alternate budded branches or straight across on opposite budded branches.
- To keep good air circulation to the inside of the plant, prune to an outside facing bud whenever possible.
- If renovating a larger woody shrub, do so over three years, taking out one-third of the branches each year.
- Take out branches that cross each other and will eventually damage one another. Doing so also increases air circulation to your plants.

Your cut should be clean, without jagged edges or tears, just above a node and gently slanted away from it.

Pruning is almost an art form. As you get better at it, you might just find yourself buying shrubs for the express purpose of pruning them. For instance, I regularly trim many broad-leaved evergreens, such as euonymus and holly, into little "trees" that make me smile in the winter. No one taught me, I just found my own way. You will too once you start trying.

I recommend:

When I'm feeling a little unsure, I consult *The American Horticultural Society Pruning and Training* by Christopher Brickell and David Joyce or, for a quicker glance, *Ortho's All About Pruning* by Judy Lowe.

Wind will cause scarring when crossed branches rub against each other. One of these crepe myrtle stems needs to go.

Still lacking confidence? Consider this: I'm a dirt-under-her-nails gardener with a taste for books and a distaste for the uber-connection of the digital age, yet I've learned how to write a bit of code for my website. I hate every minute of it, but I've learned how.

You can learn how to prune your plants, raise your own seedlings, and build skills in a discipline that you love. Who knows where you'll go from there.

VINEYARD IN TOWN

Unexpected seems an inadequate word to describe the garden of Paul Lehmann and Jeannie Goforth, tucked into the quiet end of an older city cul-de-sac in Western Maryland. Yet that's exactly what it is.

Vegetables and berries abound, as do old favorites like roses, lavender, and santolina, but all within the context of a fully operational home vineyard that has been their passion for fifteen years.

Paul, a Vietnam veteran, has been making wine since his days in the Army, but it wasn't until they moved to the city lot in 1997 that he thought about growing grapes. Larger properties in the well-known wine regions nearby were out of reach and too much to manage; however, the partly shaded, sloping lot covered in grass and squeezed between neighbors had one thing going for it: a southern exposure.

Luckily, Paul and Jeannie had something going for them too: a dogged determination to grow grapes against the odds. They cleared trees to gain a bit more sunlight, created terraces, had battles

with deer and officious city code officers, and slowly created what is now a magnificent mini vineyard that illustrates the old adage "never say never."

I visit them on a day when Cabernet Franc, Merlot, and Cabernet Sauvignon grapes hang heavily from netted rows. The fruit is a few precious weeks from harvest, and Paul treats me to a glass of his 2010 Catoctin—a 100 percent estate grown red blend. Barrel-aged for thirteen months in a back room of his basement

the warm, rich nose and smooth complexity defies most people's expectations of homemade wine. On average, the vineyard supplies them sixteen cases a year.

"At one point in my life there were those, including my parents, who said that I should be a tradesman and not even think about college because they couldn't help me," says Paul, a retired hydrologist and

geologist. "I made it happen. If experts had advised me on this vineyard and garden, they would have said to forget it; it can't be done. I very much dislike hearing that something can't be done—it's an easy way out."

Paul's days are hardly easy. In addition to his own vineyard, he manages a country vineyard nearby for a homeowner, trading labor and knowledge for the ability to stock his cellar with Traminette and Chardonnay. Between pruning, weeding, spraying, harvesting, crushing, fermenting, racking, and bottling, he works hard for that wine, but it's what he loves. There's no wine snob here, only a man working diligently at a dream.

"I'm just an ordinary guy," he asserts, as we sit surveying the vineyard and Jeannie's abundant roses and vegetable beds from the comfort of their sunroom.

"With an extraordinary garden," I add, and we all clink glasses in agreement.

SECTION THREE
MAINTAIN

9
STRIKING A BALANCE

"Oh, Adam was a gardener, and God who made him sees,
That half a proper gardener's work is done upon his knees."
—Rudyard Kipling

I'm a fanatical gardener. That means that I average two to four unpaid hours outside every day covered in dirt, talking to myself, and generally looking pretty rough. I love almost every minute of it, and will happily tack on more time whenever I can spare it. But that's just it. I can hardly spare the time I'm currently spending out there, much less add more. You probably feel the same way.

This used to bug me—a lot. At any one time in the garden, there were forty projects that I could be working on. From weeding to planting, no matter how much I was doing, I could be doing more. Yet I still had bills to pay, kids to chase, columns to write, and there was no chance of snapping my fingers and saying "Dinner on the terrace tonight Jeeves."

We all maintain a different balance of work and play in our lives. Most of us are striving for a life that gives us professional satisfaction, but still allows time for recreational activities.

There are, of course, times when we don't have a choice. Times when we must hold down two jobs just to make ends meet—or hold down those jobs and attend night classes to move a little closer to our career goals—leaving little time for anything else.

But there are also times when we *do* have a choice in this balancing act, and obsessive thinking makes us feel like we don't. That's when gardening becomes an endless chore, and that's when we begin to grow resentful. And not just

The author, calf-deep in weeds.

resentful of those who have more resources than we do, but of those around us such as spouses or children who do not share our desires and wish to use their spare time in another way.

With limited time, resources, and energy, we must set priorities and remember that we're aiming for a garden that energizes, not enervates, us.

I had to learn that the hard way.

Though it's good to always be busy out there, you don't want a garden that fills you with guilt and makes you start every sentence with "I've got to . . ." the moment you walk outside.

You don't want to grow to resent your garden.

This chapter is about helping you create a joyous balance between your garden and your life; but, I warn you, it is structured around hard truths that may have you uncomfortably wriggling in your seat. Uncomfortable or not, these are the guidelines that keep me sane in the garden, and I share them with you now hoping that they'll help you too (and you won't shoot the messenger). They are not intended to make you think rigidly, but realistically. That's the path to a garden that brings you joy.

Hard Truth Number 1:
There will never be a time when I am completely finished.

This is either going to terrify or excite you. As a novice gardener with moderate OCD tendencies, it used to scare the heck out of me. It took years of meeting other gardeners, seeing other gardens, and reading the great garden essayists to make me realize that we are not striving for a point in the future—we are living a process.

Accepting this truth frees us to enjoy our gardens. We will never be finished. The process is the point. So we do what we can, when we can, and we don't bite off more than we can chew. This starts with creating realistic expectations.

So how much time *do* you have to garden each day? Back in the planning stage I asked you this same question. A half hour? Two? Four hours on a weekend? There's no wrong answer as long as you are being truthful and matching that time to the long-term goals of your garden.

That last bit is important. If you want a major design, you have to be willing to spend

Even in the "finished" design, plants need replacing . . . and always will.

major time **creating** it and, more importantly, **maintaining** it. It's usually pretty easy to find time to create something, especially once we are in the groove. But, like cleaning the bedroom you freshly painted and decorated six months ago, the upkeep can quickly lose its appeal.

If we categorize our work in the garden under these two headings, it's easy to understand why that is.

Creation	Maintenance
Planning	Weeding
Designing	Edging
Building	Mowing
Purchasing	Organizing
Planting	Replanting
Propagating	Pruning
	Cleaning
	Spraying
	Raking
	Amending
	Dividing
	Caring for tools
	Deadheading
	Monitoring
	Protecting
	Clearing
	Repairing structures
	Trimming
	Thinning

I don't know about you, but in a perfect world with unlimited resources I'd rather be working with the first list most of the time. Creation is exciting! Forget about all those platitudes that mowing is therapeutic and weeding is cathartic. They may be perfectly true, but wouldn't you *rather* be purchasing new plants and creating new features all the time?

The problem is, resources are limited, there is no staff of gardeners to instruct, and the second list is significantly longer than the first. That's why our time in the garden can't be apportioned like this:

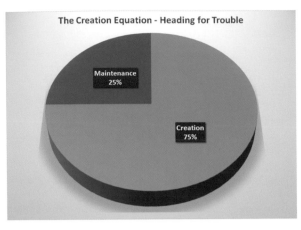

Or even this:

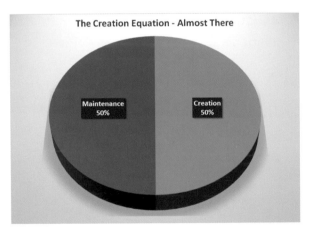

It should probably look more like this instead:

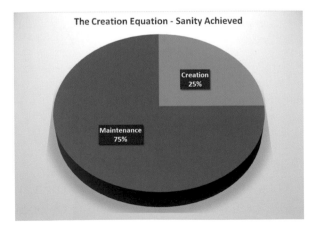

Big Dreams, Small Garden

Hard Truth Number 2:
Whatever I create, I have an obligation to maintain.

It sounds harsh, I understand. But if I am strict with myself when I am designing a new feature of my garden, and always do so with a view to maintaining it within the scope of my resources (time, money, energy), it alleviates a great deal of guilt and heartache later.

In some ways, I almost consider this an ethical issue, particularly when resources are scarce. If we commit those resources to a project and then waste them because time and nature have erased our efforts while we moved on to the next project, we're not being good stewards of those resources any more than a person who buys a new car when the brakes go out on the old one.

A nursery grower friend of mine encapsulated the whole process when she said, "The tiny shrub will grow. Those irises will need dividing. Even though you plant it today, you are growing it for tomorrow. It's a gardener's responsibility to see out his or her plan."

There are exceptions, of course. Aging heads that list, as does injury. The latter may not ever happen, but the former is inevitable and will severely curtail what we are able to do out there. Changes in our work schedules may also force new adaptations and removal of features that were once reasonable to maintain. In these cases, we have to make tough decisions before things get out of hand.

It only takes a small amount of time for rows of berries to get out of control, and then you've got a nightmare on your hands. A few minutes of weekly maintenance is a much better idea.

However, let me be clear: maintaining your garden or an area of your garden doesn't mean it has to be pillbox-hat perfect. One man's meadow is just as certainly another man's weedy lawn; and one woman's abundant cottage garden is another woman's town and country nightmare. Only you understand the vision you had for a certain area of your garden. Maintenance should be just enough to allow that vision to shine through.

Hard Truth Number 3:
If I cannot maintain it, I need to change it.

Even if we have fully considered maintenance before we create, life happens. Here are a few warning signs that life has happened to you.

1. Thinking about your garden makes you feel uneasy or stressed.
2. You've lost track of plants or areas on which you spent significant time and/or money.
3. Beds are choked with perennial weeds to a point that cultivated plants can no longer be seen.
4. Pathways are blocked and it is difficult to get from one part of the garden to another.
5. A bountiful vegetable garden remains largely unharvested.
6. You find yourself purchasing new tools and materials to replace those that have not been maintained.

If more than a few of these points make you say "Uh-oh," don't berate yourself, beat yourself up, or spend another minute thinking negatively. It's just time to make some changes to alleviate maintenance issues and have you loving your garden again. The good news is that little changes can have a significant impact without lessening your enjoyment of your garden.

For instance, if, contrary to your sister's warnings, you plant a hillside of salvia on a drip line in California's rugged foothills (never believing that opportunistic weeds will enjoy the extra water and lack of

Don't need thirty-five pounds of plums every year? It might be a good idea to forget about the plum tree and get the five pounds you want from a farmers' market instead.

heavyweight competition), only to find out you can't keep up with the weeding because you just had a baby and you're trying to run a winery; it may be time to rip out the salvia, rip out the drip line, and cover your hillside with creeping rosemary, which doesn't take prisoners and tastes great with pork loin.

Not that I'm saying that ever happened.

To my sister.

Last year.

Hard Truth Number 4:
I can't just work hard; I must also work smart.

Weeding your concrete pavers with a pointed trowel works beautifully at dusk after a summer downpour. In fact, it's almost (dare I say) cathartic after an argument with your spouse (not that that has ever happened either).

Weeding your concrete pavers under the midday sun four weeks into a drought before you have lunch and after an argument with your spouse is going to put you off gardening for the rest of your life.

Matching time, mood, energy, and environment to a task can make that task simpler and much more enjoyable. This requires the ability to think ahead *and* the ability to be flexible.

If you set aside a late-August Saturday to paint your bedroom, but the weather is a gorgeous seventy degrees when Saturday dawns, you may want to reschedule the painting for Sunday and instead hit the daylily bed that is choked with Japanese stiltgrass.

That, and call a couple of friends over for a spontaneous bottle of Malbec on the deck.

Early morning is the best time to harvest your vegetables. If you wait until you need them later in the day, you'll battle heat and bugs and harvest produce that has sustained significant water loss during the day.

Hard Truth Number 5:
What works for someone else might not work for me.

A good friend of mine is a brilliant organic gardener, and her garden is smaller than mine. If she has a pest, she handpicks it until the population is decimated. If grass is becoming a problem in her pathways, she removes the gravel, places a new layer of cardboard down, and order is restored. (Although she probably never let it get out of hand in the first place.)

I garden differently. I handpick pests like Japanese beetles and cabbage loopers and never let chemical sprays anywhere near my vegetables, but I do not have a problem with spraying my paths with an emergent weed killer in the spring—if I remember to get around to it.

Although our methods of gardening will reflect who we are and what we believe, they are also dependent on what we are growing, how much time we have, and how we are willing to spend it. Sometimes we don't know how this is going to play out until we actually start gardening. During that discovery process we might find that our ideologies are called into question or strengthened.

For instance, I don't grow common summer squash in the summer any more. The squash borer issues that I consistently encounter in the mid-Atlantic make the whole process a pain of mammoth proportions. I'm not willing to spray my vegetables with neonicotinoids, and the barrier methods espoused by the organic journals just don't work consistently enough for me. I could spend my summer frustrated and angry (and spending too much time on the issue), or I can grow an Italian trailing variety that is very resistant to the pest and takes less of my time.

I choose the latter option, but I also grow a late batch of summer squash seedlings when the borer wasps have stopped flying. The squash does terrific in a warm fall but not so well during a cold, wet one. Sometimes I get zucchini and sometimes I don't, but I don't kill myself over it just because everyone else around me is willing to rewrap their squash stems with aluminum foil every morning.

Do what works for you and your garden.

After a long day of working in the flower beds, you may feel that a pre-emergent herbicide on the pathways is the difference between exhaustion and enjoyment.

Hard Truth Number 6: I need to research the plants I choose to cultivate.

Plant height and spread are rarely exaggerated. If anything, they are often understated by growers/nurseries who want you to feel like you could, possibly, make room for something.

This is going to catch you out many times in your gardening career and create maintenance woes for you down the line, but when it's a marketer's fault, it's completely understandable.

However, when you—presumably of sound mind and body—plant a twelve-foot spreading forsythia next to your front door path under the expectation that you will prune it every May without fail (cross your heart hope to die), you are setting yourself up for a big headache.

Soon that forsythia will fulfill all promises of growth. But what's more, the twenty-foot rambling rose you chose to grow on the south side of the house will too, as will the trumpet vine crawling over the pergola and now seeding into the beds. Meanwhile, the artistic pruning you swore you'd do on the standard Japanese maple is now three seasons behind, and you're afraid the tree might slap you if you touch it.

Your garden has now become 99 percent maintenance and 1 percent creation, and your weekends are spent wrestling angry (and sometimes armed) shrubs.

A bit of research can prevent these headaches before they happen. There really are dwarf forsythias. A climbing rose will not behave like a rambler, a dwarf Japanese maple won't need constant pruning, and a well-behaved clematis will clothe your pergola with well-behaved flowers and seed heads.

Sometimes research is as easy as talking to experienced gardeners in your area. If they roll their eyes or clutch their chests when you mention a certain plant you want to try, you may want to ask for suggestions or hit the books again.

This climbing hydrangea looks fantastic, but comes with an attached gardener in this high-end garden. Putting one on the side of your own house means constant trimming. If you've got time, great. If not, you're in for trouble.

Hard Truth Number 7: I'm doing a great thing.

Okay, maybe that's not such a hard truth. But on days when I'm feeling overwhelmed, underappreciated, tired, cranky, and ready to chuck it all in (and believe me this happens more often than you'd think), it's something I can come back to.

When I'm in my garden, the connection I'm making with the earth is one of the most primal, and life-giving. And if someone steps into my garden and feels that connection and is

Take a minute to see the small miracles in your garden, particularly the ones you didn't plan.

inspired to create it in their own life, I've just done a great thing.

A COMMUNITY GARDEN

Two minutes in the animated, enthusiastic company of David Muns and I find myself wanting to start my own community garden.

Except I already have, and I know how much work is involved.

From his deep suntan and ragged T-shirt, you might be able to guess at how many hours he volunteers in managing the one hundred and thirty-five plot community garden in Central Maryland that involves more than one hundred families, but you'd almost certainly fall short.

Why does he do it? "The wonderful people," says David with a smile as he hands me a cherry tomato from an heirloom variety in one of his own plots. "People garden here for all sorts of reasons. It gets them away from what they're doing and reconnects them," he explains.

As we walk past beds that showcase a myriad of gardening techniques, I ask if it's more about connection than food sometimes. David nods his head, but is quick to point out that fifteen of their garden beds funnel hundreds of pounds of produce into the local food banks, because sometimes *it is* just about food.

The land upon which the garden sits belongs to a local paper, *The Frederick News-Post*, a family owned business that enthusiastically supported the idea when David and other volunteers proposed it three years ago.

Full-time teachers, custodians, middle-managers, and their children all garden here in a wonderful mix of ethnicities that expose other gardeners to unusual vegetables like fenugreek or bitter melon. Recently a local nursing home built waist-high salad tables to allow their residents to once again plunge their hands in the soil. "We're a community of like-minded people," David says of those who choose to garden here. "Not everyone has space for a garden at home. Some don't have full sun. We provide that."

The garden provides more than just that. David and other volunteers have constructed an incredible system for irrigating with reclaimed water, a huge shed for community tools, seating for a garden meal, and recently four beehives to encourage pollination and provide honey for those who work them.

Community gardens have flourished over the last decade, as fewer people have had access to property. Compounding that problem is the very real issue of younger generations no longer being taught basic concepts in order to raise their own food. A community garden fills

those gaps, not only providing space to a prospective gardener, but also one-on-one relationships with others who have knowledge to share.

The FNP garden is no exception. It's community gardening at its best, and an outlet for those who ache for more than just a few pots on their doorstep. The hours that David spends making that possible are more than just a gift to his fellow gardeners, they're a gift to his community as a whole.

10
MAKING IT EASIER

"Try not to beat back the current, yet be not drowned in its waters."
—John Milton Hay

Creating and maintaining a beautiful garden is not easy. Anyone who tells you so is selling something—not least of all a book. But we can certainly make the process of maintenance *easier*. In the last chapter we considered big-picture guidelines that can help us structure our time and efforts, alert us if we're spending too much time out there, and take steps to correct the situation if we are.

So, assuming that the basic structure of your garden is in balance with your life, in this chapter we'll get in the trenches. Literally. With some of the best day-to-day tips and tricks out there to help you maintain the garden that you have grown to love without an army of undergardeners at your disposal.

These tips are broken into generalized categories because every garden is unique; we don't all have lawns, and we don't all have vegetable beds. Across the nation, we garden in different zones and with different plant palettes. Yet there are constants in any gardener's life. We all have to weed, water, mulch, take care of our soil and our tools, and deal with the challenges that pests and wildlife throw at us all season.

In each of these categories, always consider timing to maximize your effort. Whether it's the time of day, the weather, or the season, many chores in the garden are made easier by matching the chore to an efficient time in which to do it.

For instance:

Time of day	→	Watering in the morning to limit evaporation
Weather	→	Weeding after a light rain
Season	→	Organizing tools and the shed in the winter when tasks are lessened

A little thought and a bit of flexibility when it comes to timing allows you to take advantage of all the opportunities in your garden, creating less work in the long run for a busy gardener.

- Many maintenance problems can be avoided by maintaining a healthy, living soil that provides nutrients and retains available moisture, yet drains freely. Put your efforts here and healthier plants will suffer from fewer disease and pest problems in the long run.

- To see what your soil is actually missing, conduct a cheap soil test at the start of each growing season. Don't forget to also check your soil's pH (acid/alkaline). You may find that it's too high or too low, which will prevent certain plants from absorbing the nutrients your soil test is telling you are present.

- Do not work soil when it is very wet. Compaction problems will ultimately result, destroying the soil's oxygen-holding capabilities.

- To prevent compaction in the early spring when garden beds are being intensively worked, lay down boards to stand on while you work.

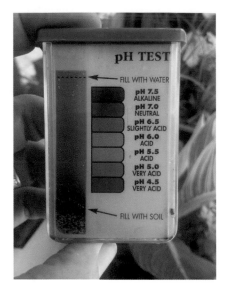

You won't know what your soil needs unless you test it. Doing so is cheap . . . and illuminating.

- Amendments to specifically improve a soil's fertility should be done in the early spring so nutrients such as nitrogen are not lost over a long winter.

- However, make amendments to your soil's pH in the autumn, so the soil has a chance to adjust before the new growing season begins.

- Amendments of organic material to improve porosity and moisture retention can be made at any time.

- Seasonal stress is heavier on container-grown plants, and they need more in the way of nutrients and good soil. Make sure your pots are filled with the best soil and are continually fed during the growing season.

- If you're mixing your own potting soil, put the lighter materials, such as perlite, at the bottom of the container and the heavier ones on top. As you mix, the heavier materials naturally move downward and make the job much faster.

Maples search out every available source of water and can destroy friable beds and septic lines. They'll even steal from containers.

- Never underestimate the root spread of a large tree, which can easily move beyond its drip line. If your beds look parched and nutrient deficient in spite of all you're doing and you've got a large tree nearby, dig down and see if there's a thief in the soil. You may want to adjust the design of your bed or change the planting scheme.

Weeding

- Always go outside with water in a flask or bottle. Thirst makes us grumpy.
- If you use gloves, consider lightweight latex or nitrile gloves so you can have a better feel and grip on weeds. Take them off carefully and you can reuse them.
- Wear trousers with good back and leg pockets or, even better, an apron with pockets. I'm a big fan of the ultimate weeding apron: the Roo (www.rooapron.com).
- Stop irritations before they happen. If you have a problem with flying insects, start your weeding with a netted hat on your head. If you get hungry quickly, go out there on a fuller stomach.
- Leave an upturned garden trug in strategic places in your garden. It inspires you to fill it up.
- Weed damp, not wet, soil.
- Tackle one area at a time for a sense of satisfaction; when you feel like leaving it, take a drink of water instead and fight the sensation until the area is finished.
- Weed before they seed! For instance, if you're planning on weeding a large area of chickweed but notice another where the bitter cress is starting to set seed, change your plan for the day.
- Keep a small garbage bag in your apron. If you come across a weed that spreads through stolons (like Bermuda grass) or a weed that is covered in seed heads, put it in the bag, and when you're finished for the day, *throw it in the garbage can.*

If you live where gnats make your life a misery, keep a gnat hat in a handy place to grab for garden chores.

Breakfast is served—at no cost to me and at great benefit to my garden.

Making It Easier

- Use a Dutch hoe or regular hoe to cut the heads off annual weeds in dry soil, killing the weed.
- Use a sharp-pointed trowel. A three- or four-inch mason's trowel is one of the best tools you can buy to get at the root of a weed and provide a flat scraping surface.
- While not practical for every gardener, there is no greater motivation for weeding than having a few backyard hens that are thrilled to receive whatever you dig up— and make eggs and compost out of it!
- If you're dealing with a particularly pernicious weed that you wish to spray, cut the bottom out of a one- or three-quart black plastic pot, put it over the weed, and spray it within this shield, protecting the plants around it.

Watering

- Enrich your soil wherever possible. Soil filled with organic matter retains more moisture and lessens the watering load.
- Water in the morning, setting your plants up for a hot day ahead and limiting evaporation.
- Pound cheap grade stakes into the corners of your beds to act as hose guides so you don't break your plants while trying to water them.
- If your hose spigot is in a difficult place to access, use a short (strong) length of hose with a valve at the end to locate it somewhere more convenient. Use long garden staples to affix it to the ground and cover with mulch for camouflage. Regularly check the hose for leaks and disassemble for the winter.
- Rain barrels at the end of drain spouts are not only environmentally friendly, but highly convenient when a water spigot is unavailable.
- If you have very little time to water, avoid using containers for plants.

Not all rain barrels have to be plastic eyesores. Consider old barrels with covers or barrels made with aesthetics in mind.

- If you have many containers, arrange plants with similar moisture needs together so watering is easier.
- Consider using plastic or glazed ceramic pots, which retain moisture longer than terracotta.
- In areas where it is difficult to bring a hose, use water spikes (such as *Plant Nanny*) to keep an inverted bottle filled with water, directing it at your plants as they need it.

Plants transpire more freely as light and heat levels increase. A good soaking won't bring these geraniums around, but a nighttime respite from high temperatures will.

- Understand that many plants, such as hydrangea and leucanthemum, will droop in the heat of midday as moisture is released from leaves (transpiration). They do not necessarily need watering.
- Try not to drop your watering spray heads on the ground. It prematurely wears them out.
- Consider installing a drip irrigation system to preserve precious water and save time. Your initial outlay of effort and money will be returned with interest by the savings in those same areas later. Such a system may also allow you to responsibly grow plants you otherwise couldn't keep hydrated.
- If you have a very dry area of your garden and can't invest in a drip irrigation system right now, consider using soaker hoses under mulch instead.
- Plant with watering in mind. Site plants where they will do best, not where they need life support in the form of a watering wand.
- In perpetually dry climates, get familiar with the term "xeriscaping" and specifically plant for your environment—reducing or actually eliminating the need for additional water.
- Use mulch to keep in moisture and keep soil cooler than bare earth.

Mulching

- Mulching does not necessarily require traditional double-shred bark. Any organic material can be used as long as it is free of weed seeds. Consider grass clippings, pine needles, leaf compost, straw, garden compost, and well-rotted manure.
- Always think in terms of seed load when it comes to mulch. Make sure bales of straw are kept outside for a season or two before using. Don't use fresh manure, and make sure that your compost is well-rotted before using it. If it's free, it's best to let it sit for a season just to be sure.

- Putting a layer of cardboard down beneath your mulch will further suppress weeds.
- Two to three inches of mulch is *plenty,* unless you are beginning a new bed or trying to kill existing turf or weeds.
- When a large amount of mulch is being delivered, put down a tarp to make cleanup the work of a minute. Use a small tarp near garden beds as well.
- Setting a garden trug on its side and using a hand cultivator to quickly scoop mulch into it is often faster than shoveling. As a bonus, you can sprinkle larger amounts into beds at one time, holding the trug on your hip.
- If you have a great deal of small plants that need mulch around them, cover them with upturned pots, and then dump your mulch. It's much faster than moving around them.

Double-shred is not the only game in town. Consider all your options, particularly in a vegetable garden.

- Sometimes just taking a hand fork and lightly scraping the top of old mulch is enough to break the hard crust that has formed and visually rejuvenate it for another season.
- "Living mulches" of annual plants are being used more and more these days in organic production to reduce soil erosion and enrich soils. Consider a cover crop in your vegetable beds, especially those that you are not using for a season. Cover crops like winter rye can sometimes provide a bonus crop, while crown vetch will help fix nitrogen in the soil and crowd out noxious weeds. Research the crop carefully, as some can create more problems if not utilized correctly.

Once the weeds are removed, a layer or two of cardboard with three inches of mulch will make it much easier to keep the weeds under control in this area.

Pest control

- Schedule time every day to walk through your garden and scan for pests. This can be while you're enjoying your morning coffee or after dinner in the evening. If you can be disciplined and not check social media, email, and texts, bring your phone or a small digital camera to take pictures of pests for later identification. Understanding what's going on is half the battle.
- Take a small plastic container filled with soapy water with you and go on a treasure hunt for larger pests like Japanese beetles or tomato hornworms.
- If you're using organic or chemical sprays, have the right ones mixed and conveniently on hand. Then when you see pest loads becoming problematic, you can immediately deal with them rather than waiting until you can organize yourself.
- Sometimes, eliminating pest issues isn't just about battles in the border. For instance, if you have a hard time with squash bug or borer, you can a) stop growing squash, b) grow a resistant variety, or c) grow it earlier or later than the traditional season with frost protection.
- Use duct tape to remove the hard rows of tiny eggs on the underside of plants laid by numerous species of vegetable-munching bugs. It works like a charm!
- If applicable, use backyard chickens to rid your spring vegetable patch of overwintering bugs and many weed seeds. A win-win for all of you.

Sometimes, Mother Nature takes care of it for you. This tomato hornworm is currently being parasitized by hundreds of braconid wasp cocoons and doesn't have a long life ahead of it.

This tarp is being used over two seasons to kill weeds without using herbicides.

Making It Easier

- The sun is a powerful tool. Use black plastic tacked over problem areas to give pests and weeds the worst sunburn of their life.
- Manage your expectations and you won't feel frantic. You're not going to have perfect vegetables or perfect flowers. You only need to act when populations are visibly growing and threatening the vitality of the plant.

Shed/workyard

- Whether your shed or work area is large or small, organization is crucial to saving time. If your work area is on display in your garden, it's also crucial to have a pleasing design. Train yourself to put things away.

- Use old totes to hold go-to planting materials, such as soil, perlite, sand, gravel, and peat moss, allowing you to save money by buying in bulk and keeping materials conveniently at hand.

- Old five-gallon buckets work beautifully for holding bulk fertilizers and keeping them fresh. Use some camouflage spray paint on them if you don't have a shed and don't want them too visible in your potting area.

- Set up tool stations in your garden by putting up old mailboxes and stands that can be painted an attractive color. Stay disciplined and keep the tools for that area in the mailbox. A climbing vine like clematis makes them even more beautiful.

A repurposed mailbox post with a box made of scrap wood and supplies makes a terrific tool station and hose rack for a remote corner of the garden.

- Find an old patio table and use it to create a potting station against a wall or fence. With a bit of stain or paint, you can use cast-offs to create a functional, beautiful space.
- Continually go through your stacks of plastic pots, keeping those that are of high quality for transplants and seedlings, and recycling those that are just taking up room in the shed.
- Invest in a small, no-frills bench grinder and place it somewhere convenient in your basement, garage, or shed. Then, when the mood strikes you to sharpen your spades, shovels or loppers, the grinder is always at the ready. Bench grinders are cheap—certainly much cheaper than throwing away tools.

THE *ILLUSION* OF NEAT

The very best trick I use on a constant basis applies to all gardens, regardless of size, shape, or scope. When I'm up against it, when the garden is a mess, when friends are coming over or I'm having a party, and I don't know where to start, *I create the illusion of "neat."* It's surprisingly simple to do:

- Mow any grass you have.
- Lightly sprinkle bare patches of garden beds with fresh mulch or straw.
- Remove fallen and dead materials, such as branches and twigs.
- If time permits, go over your edges with a weed whacker.

Think of it the same way you think of doing a quick clean in your house when someone is coming over. No deep cleaning, but you'll run the vacuum, stack the dishes, and pick up the dirty socks. It makes a huge difference to the overall look of the space.

Yes, it may be chaotic deep in the heart of those beds, but tidying the periphery up makes it look like you're totally in control.

GARDENING AGAINST THE GRAIN: AN HOA GARDEN

Sheryl Massaro is a painter. Her canvas jacket is spattered with the greens and browns indicative of the pastoral landscapes that hang on her walls and in nearby galleries in Frederick County, Maryland.

But Sheryl is also a gardener and a writer. Six years ago, ed by a desire to own a home after years of townhome and condo living, she bought into a popular development—a development under the auspices of an HOA.

Developments managed by community housing associations, or HOAs, have become increasingly popular in the ast two decades. But when you sign on that line for a new home with the benefits of community amenities and common area maintenance, you are also handing over the freedom to do whatever you want with your garden, whenever you want.

For those desirous of low-maintenance foundation plantings and a park for the kids, this arrangement works just fine.

But it just wasn't working for Sheryl. Though she loved her new neighbors, she wasn't crazy about a boring landscape populated with the holy trinity of the modern development: lawn, arborvitae, and magenta azaleas.

She wanted a garden. A real garden with paths, drifts of perennials, specimen plants, and a place to sit and take it all in on warm summer nights. No lawn, no weed and feed, and absolutely no azaleas.

Those familiar with the militant nature of some housing associations would have advised her to move . . . again. But Sheryl was not to be discouraged. She really hated mowing. She really loved her neighbors. She decided to play by the rules, but with a strategy that relied on offense, not defense.

The HOA board was presented with a simple landscape plan that Sheryl had a reliable local nursery draw up. She spent hours creating

a document that listed all plants, provided thumbnail photos, and gave the sizes of the plants once they matured. She provided her credentials as a newly minted Master Gardener, and she made sure that she was present and available on the night of the vote.

"I made it as easy for them as possible," she recalls. "I anticipated all the questions and took away all the little decisions that could hang up the process."

She got her garden. Four years later, it is a flourishing mix of perennials, annuals, evergreens and ground covers—not all of which were on the original plan, but all of which are delightful.

Pebbled pathways lead the visitor from the driveway to the front door, where ironwork chairs allow the weary resident gardener to sit after a long day weeding.

"Being in my garden allows me to get reacquainted with my neighbors or get to know new people," she says. "It's a great conversation starter."

It's also a great influencer. A year ago, motivated by the beauty and charm of her garden, her next-door neighbors went through the same process with the HOA and now have their own stunning no-mow landscape. Other neighbors are contemplating the same.

"That's got to make you proud," I say, remarking on the two gardens complementing one another through a white picket fence. Sheryl smiles and nods. "It was worth the hassle," she says.

11

ENLISTING THE TROOPS

"No man is an island."
—John Donne

Every other year or so, I am able to travel back to visit my family on the other side of the United States. My mother plans the thrift store shopping, my sisters plan the wine tasting tours, my brother plans the fishing trips, but my father plans the projects. He knows that the only thing I like doing more than a garden or household project is doing that project with someone else.

In fact, I enjoy it so much that I'll gladly spend much of my vacation doing just that.

I've always enjoyed working with other people in the garden—that is, until I had my own children who behaved very much as I did as a child: complaining, taking numerous bathroom breaks, and utilizing a system of timekeeping that would confuse Stephen Hawking.

But more about that later.

Many hands make light work. Not just in the amount of work completed, but in the camaraderie and companionship of many minds focused on the same goal, which is sometimes as simple as getting to the end and opening a beer. And when you feel overwhelmed by a big project in the garden, finding someone to help you can be the trigger to get started and keep going.

Sometimes those outside projects are fun creation projects, like building a new shed or laying a flagstone patio. But much of the time we just need help with big maintenance projects,

The author (center), with her siblings and father, building a swing set many years ago.

like *re-roofing* the shed, or *re-grouting* the flagstone patio . . . or getting the weeding done before both of them disappear.

And we don't have the resources to call the landscaping crew and write a hefty check.

This is where, once again, our garden gives us an opportunity to significantly connect with others. You may think that I'm cleverly spinning the act of getting a bit of help in the garden, but I'm actually very serious.

Let's look at two ways of not only finding help with your projects, but through those actions, strengthening relationships, building skills, and leaving a lasting effect on the lives of our friends and our families.

Help from friends—the work party

There's something about big projects that cries out for a cooler of something cold, a weekend afternoon, and a lot of hands on deck. The concept of a work party is not new, but it takes a bit of management and a willingness to stay committed.

A successful group usually involves four or five households, requires one day a month, and allows you to get large jobs done that may have been on the back burner for some time. Work is followed by a potluck lunch; and, depending on age, children are

The best combination: friends, food, and a hard day's work.

either encouraged to help or looked after by rotating members of the group.

Martin Gross and Andrea Goldstein, homesteaders in Western Maryland, have been part of a successful work party for the last ten years. They've built friendships along with raised beds and French drains, and, most importantly, modeled the great benefits of community cooperation for their young children.

"We try to work on projects that are long lasting, but sometimes it's just as simple as helping out with maintenance chores when one member is overwhelmed," says Martin of the process. "It's cool to look at something in the garden and think, 'Oh yeah, that was a work party project.' It's a tangible memory of the day."

How does it work?

An example work party might meet every month on, say, the third Saturday. The household that is hosting should have a good idea beforehand of what they wish to accomplish and have the materials and specific tools available as necessary, as well as give members a heads-up to bring tools that they might have at home. Digging trenches, roofing sheds, installing electric fences, clearing brush . . . the project possibilities are endless.

Plan the work to take three to four hours, perhaps from nine in the morning to one in the afternoon, ending with a potluck lunch. Commit to an end time, so members don't feel as if they have to stay or work a little more after the meal.

It's important to stay with four or five households. If you have too many people, not only will the group become unwieldy, but you may find yourself committing the same amount of time per year and getting less done at your own place.

Though it may seem a little rigid, keeping strong guidelines allows everyone to understand exactly what is expected of them. For as much as this is about enjoying your friends and

Some may know how to build a deck, others may be learning, but all are committed to the project at hand.

Enlisting the Troops

making new ones, it's also about getting work done, and our time is precious. Make sure that the commitment is understood, as hard feelings can result from members that consistently have problems with scheduling.

When deciding who your party will involve, invite friends that have a work ethic similar to your own. Skills can always be taught. In fact, according to Andrea, the learning process is one of the most valuable benefits of a work party. "When one of the households wanted to build a French drain, we all had to learn a new skill," she notes. "It was so instructive, and such a useful project, that we've built four more since!"

Don't try to match size of property or size of muscles; there are jobs to be done on every property, regardless of size, and I for one am living proof that you can't judge a book by its cover.

If you have a large network of friends, I sympathize that it can be hard to include some people over others, but you'll actually be surprised how many people might be thankful to be left off the list when they realize it's not just about beer in the garden, but a formal commitment to work one day a month, whether it's bitter January or the lusty month of May.

If you don't have a large network of friends who might be interested, consider asking neighbors and building your community ties while you build your cold frames!

Another alternative

If you like to work with others but don't want the structure and obligation of a work party, instead ask gardener friends to trade time with you in each other's garden. We could all use a helping hand to hold a two-by-twelve while we nail, or a post while we backfill, and the company of another gardener keeps our spirits high.

I've traded time for weeding, deck building, shed painting, and frantic night-before-the-party scrambling. There's usually a lot of jokes flying around with the dirt, and the after-

Some jobs are not just easier, but also more enjoyable shared with friends.

noon's work almost always ends with a drink at dusk in the quiet company of a friend.

Such an informal arrangement works really well for my husband and I as a couple, for as much as I love the formal commitment of work parties, he loves a bit more freedom to give his help when and where he can.

Help at home—mentoring our children

If you don't have children, you can skip right over this section, or you can read it as a bit of social commentary.

Why do we completely ignore the help that is right under our noses?

Because in order to access it, we have to step up to the plate and do some serious parenting, and the alternative is, quite frankly, easier.

In our modern world, children spend more and more time indoors and very little time outside. This is not breaking news. Our childhoods bear about as much resemblance to those of our children as Bear Grylls does to Kim Kardashian.

Exercise is structured, often expensive, and always involves a parental chauffeuring service.

A memory of Tom Sawyer days

Though we remember performing hot, sweaty, and decidedly un-fun garden chores, or helping our parents with a big project for a bit of extra spending money, we are hesitant to involve our children in the same way: too quick to acquiesce when the whining begins and mildly uncomfortable with the visions of sweatshops that our children are happy to conjure with their dramatic renditions of heatstroke.

We allow ourselves to believe that today's generation is somehow different, and we give in to the temptation that generations before us successfully fought: the aching desire to just do the job ourselves and save a huge amount of aggravation.

But what are we losing in the process? More importantly, what are our children losing?

Working with your kids in the garden not only shares the workload, but it's also a memorable bonding experience for all of you.

Kids are capable—and proud to be.

Enlisting the Troops

Giving children purpose

Bill Roberson, an expert in child development and the enrollment director and parent educator at the Sierra Waldorf school in Jamestown, California, has a few thoughts on that one.

I first encountered Roberson and this wonderful school when I visited during a Michaelmas celebration. Children ranging in age from three to thirteen were preparing for their parents and relatives to visit the school that day. The kindergarten class had spent much of the morning preparing a vegetable soup and setting tables for their guests.

Tables set by the kindergarten class of the Sierra Waldorf School on a warm September day are ready for the vegetable soup made from the bounty of the school's garden.

Not only had the vegetables been grown and harvested by the children in the large school garden, but under the supervision of adults, little hands had cut up those vegetables, cooked them, and made bread to accompany the feast.

"Every child . . . wants to feel that they are a 'member,' to be known and to be included." Roberson told me. "We are members of the human community, and we are also members of the world of nature . . . In engaging in natural processes, children find a reflection of their own development. They also have the experience of seeing where food comes from and how we tend to its growth."

I felt tears prick my eyes as I watched boys and girls hanging over the top of a board fence in conversation with one another, they themselves observing a fellow twelve-year-old take a

Sometimes it takes seeing others' trust in kids to realize what our own kids can do with a little encouragement.

low branch off a tree with a pruning saw while another hoed the ground nearby. Electronic devices were not in attendance.

Anyone who has observed the steady decline of conversation between children growing up in the digital age will understand why I needed a moment to compose myself.

Here were children with purpose, children trusted with tools. Children performing necessary jobs and allowed to problem solve as the branch bent under its weight, the saw became stuck, and little voices rang out with solutions.

"Nursery students and kindergarteners at our school use saws, hammers, shovels, and rakes, always with supervision close by. Proper use and care of those tools is modeled and taught," Roberson explained. "In general, children use these tools properly with great enthusiasm and enjoyment. Real tools for real work that allows children yet another opportunity to experience meaningful membership in a group."

Such a system flies in the face of modern helicopter parenting, where children are not expected to think for themselves, to solve problems, face consequences, and, most importantly,

Enlisting the Troops

take risks. Yet giving children ownership in the garden and an appreciation for the work it takes to maintain it allows them the ability to participate in the home economy and become *producers* rather than passive consumers.

How do we start?

Even if we understand why, *how* do we as parents mired in a helicopter culture give up control? How do we take the first steps in entrusting our children with jobs we know we can do ourselves more efficiently, more carefully, and probably with a lot less aggravation?

Roberson gave me a Kobayashi Issa haiku in reply . . .

> inch by inch
> little snail
> climb Mount Fuji

. . . and followed it with another very sound piece of advice: "Being prepared is the key. Foresee the chore all the way to the end and set boundaries that will assure success and a feeling of mastery."

That means giving children a job with a beginning and an end—not just a certain number of minutes on a timer. It means being present and involved while your children are working, not checking your own device from the sidelines.

Roberson shared an example of working with his own daughter in this way:

> *When Piper was around two and a half years old, I built a rock border in the garden. I was using a big wheelbarrow to transport football-size rocks and needed smaller rocks to fill in chinks in the short wall. I got a small wheelbarrow for Piper and ran a string about 12 inches from the ground down the two sides of the planted row I'd be going down so she had a clear visual cue of where to roll her barrow.*
>
> *Her load was light, and she was able to manage the trip down the row because she already had a sense of her center of gravity and could right an imbalance. She would even rearrange her load for better balance all on her own.*
>
> *I knew there would be some challenge for her to stay within the string boundary, but I figured I could repair any damage done. She did great, wiped out a few radishes, but nothing major, and was very pleased with herself. She had the opportunity to imitate real work, to meet appropriate expectations, and gain more of a sense of her own resourcefulness. It worked because I saw that she had the capacity, was ready for a challenge, and, most of all, I trusted she could do it.*

Children learn from example, and it is never too late to implement little changes, gradually modifying what Roberson refers to as "the rhythm of a family's life."

Give a child a fish

Though I don't claim to be a child development expert, I will share with you that my children were expected to do their own laundry at eight years old. They were taught to make basic meals by ten and had a night of the week when they were in charge of dinner.

Now they help me weed, have their own garden plots, build structures, clear brush, stack wood, and help take care of a large flock of chickens.

I have a neighbor and friend to thank for opening my eyes years ago to what children were capable of by the example of her own children. It stood in stark contrast to the cultural example all around me, but it felt right, so I ran with it, allowing me to transition my focus from doing *for* them all the time (as we must in the early days of parenting), to helping them do for *themselves*.

Last year, my daughter helped me install rain barrels and build raised beds. She learned how to use a drill, a screwdriver, a saw, and her own initiative. She still had a phone in her back pocket, but there is compromise in any successful partnership.

Remember, inch by inch. You don't get there all at once. Start with these three steps:

- **Let them know that you believe them to be capable**—This does not require showering them in positive statements every two seconds; kids are smart, they know when they're being worked. Treat them in a loving, straightforward manner.
- **Shelve your fear**—Understand that children have a tendency to take risks to recognize their limits, but they also have a healthy sense of self-preservation. Allowing a child to use a pair of pruning shears with supervision does not mean that he will instantly see if he can cut off his finger. If you see unacceptable behavior, intervene immediately and dole out consequences.
- **Be a role model**—If you're not modeling the work, you can't expect them to know how to do it or get excited about doing it, particularly if you're talking on the phone or have your face in your laptop. As time goes on you'll be able to work in other areas while they get on with separate tasks, but why not work together? It's so much more rewarding.

A reality check

Does all this advice mean that my children are angels?

Oh, heck no.

My gorgeous little sandy-haired helpers are now teenagers. My children whine. They'd sleep until noon if I wasn't paying attention. They try and negotiate how long they are going to work outside. They sneak their phones. They move like molasses. They bicker with each other, and my eldest thinks I don't know that his pet name for me is Emperor Palpatine.

But they know we're serious. *We're seriously not going to budge.* So, if they whine, we have consequences, and then they get on with it. And slowly, over the course of their childhood and our sanity, we are making progress.

I know in my heart it's one of the greatest gifts we can give them (and one they won't thank us for until they are well into adulthood): the opportunity to gain skills, to solve problems, to trust in their own abilities.

And, as their skill levels have grown, my husband and I now have a very capable crew out there. They know to pull weeds by the roots, put their tools away, drive a lawn mower, back up a trailer, provide a strong pair of hands on building projects, and, as an added bonus, they know how to make me a cup of tea when I'm too exhausted to even boil water. They truly are valuable members of our family unit, not just kids along for the ride.

I'm thankful that we never had the resources for maids and cooks and gardeners to raise them any differently. They understand that we have to work hard for what we want, and that sometimes we still don't get it so we must put our minds toward finding another way. This can only help them as adults when the playing field feels a little uneven.

Yes, it's tough. Sometimes it's inconvenient. If you are not a patient soul, you're going to do some mental struggling. But, truly, it's our duty to our children, and, in many ways, to the world.

Connecting through the garden

You can do it all yourself. You can beat yourself up and proudly state that you did it your way, or you can reach out and bring others in. They'll remember you for it, whether as teacher or friend; and every time you look around and see all that has been accomplished through the cooperation of others, you'll remember them.

It's incredible how much can be achieved through the work of many hands. Here, a community garden has begun with a lot of community spirit.

A FAMILY AFFAIR

Steven Biggs has always believed in including his kids in his garden. So much so that last year he handed over control of his precious tomato patch to his ten-year-old daughter, Emma.

It was a gamble that paid off. Seven hundred tomatoes later, she's expanding it this year onto the roof, where she hopes to grow one thousand. She's also blogging and speaking about it to other children who want to get into gardening at www.growgardeners.com.

A freelance writer located in a suburb of Ontario, Canada, Steven is the author of

Gardening with Kids. His garden is on a small lot in an ordinary neighborhood next to houses that don't garden, and he has one crucial piece of advice to share with parents, whether they have a tenth of an acre or ten: "Be a role model."

"When I'm outside, they're outside," the soft-spoken father of three tells me. "It's easy to get too serious with things being just right, but you have to come at it a different way—as play. It should be fun and instructive."

He doesn't believe in all the apparatus we think we need to make that possible: the child-sized plastic tools that don't dig well, the matching gloves that get lost. These things are indicative of a consumer culture that slots certain activities into certain time periods, makes them reliant on specific supplies, and inevitably makes them less accessible.

"Gardening is easier than that," he says.

Steven also believes in the need for risk in a child's play life, allowing them to understand their own limits and perhaps challenge them. In a Canadian school system that has just forbidden the throwing of snowballs and building of snow forts on school property, it's getting harder and harder to find these opportunities for kids. Steven maintains that "this is where parents have to step up."

Being outside with your children and including them in the home economy through the garden is one such way. Especially if you garden on the roof.

Steven has limited space, and several years ago he turned to the microclimate of his flat garage roof to grow vegetables. With the help of self-watering containers, he is able to grow all the heat lovers the family adores, like melons, peppers, and squash.

"It's a great use of an otherwise ugly space," he explains. "And, it makes people think about what they can do."

It's certainly making Emma think about what she can do. If she hits her goal of one thousand tomatoes this year, her dad has no doubt she'll have even loftier goals for the next growing season.

SECTION FOUR
ENJOY

12

LIVING IN THE EDEN YOU HAVE CREATED

"What is this life if, full of care,
We have no time to stand and stare."
—WH Davies

Gardening is about process, with the promise of result hanging like a gourmet carrot on the end of a very long stick.

Some gardeners understand this instinctively; how else could the ratio of labor to result be justified to a rational mind? Things aren't always pretty out there, yet still we toil on, strengthening the connection between ourselves and our outside world as we battle this pest or acquire that plant—or create a jaw-dropping entrance while our back garden disappears in a tangle of vines.

But sometimes the avid gardener gets too caught up in the finish line sprint and forgets to take time to enjoy the small snatches of result all around him. There, with the lawn trimmed, the deck decked, the beds overflowing, and the air heavy with scent, he feels vaguely and surprisingly unsatisfied, and the entire point of the exercise is lost.

Our gardens are meant to be enjoyed. There is no sense in building a deck that you only use twice a year. Quite frankly, it's easier and cheaper to rent a pavilion in a park. Similarly, a corner of your garden devoted to night-blooming ornamentals is pretty pointless if you only get down there during the day to weed the paving stones and plan the next garden room.

In a result-driven world, we can perhaps be forgiven for looking at our gardens as a task to be finished and *then* enjoyed, but without a change of perspective, you're heading for trouble. As I stressed in Chapter 9, it's never going to be finished all at once.

Don't panic if you didn't realize that when you started this book. If the process were different, the gardener's heart within you would tire and become bored. Our challenge as gardeners is not only to create and work our gardens, but to enjoy them as they evolve in the micro and the macro over time.

And, don't forget, that means helping others enjoy them too.

In the following sections, I've put together a few ways to do just that. Pick one, pick several, and gradually train yourself to slow down and observe the beauty around you, for it *is* a question of training oneself to approach the garden in a different way.

First, a quick caveat

Lifestyle and garden magazines, TV shows, websites, and books, as inspiring as they are, can contribute to the sense of result over process. As you read through the following strategies for enjoying your garden, do not keep comparing yourself to gardens prepped for a photo shoot.

Do not let the perfect be the enemy of the good.

A chance to relax

- Find the best views in your garden and install a seat to take advantage of them. Remember, a view is not necessarily staring at mountains or oceans or vast stretches of Montana sky. It's something that you find pleasing, that others will find pleasing, a scent, a lush environment, an intricate pattern, a quiet corner.
- A seat is a destination for yourself and your visitors. It quietly whispers "this is a place to rest for a while." And we do.
- Seats don't need to be permanent, which is good, because views often aren't permanent either. The bluebells and lily of the valley clustered around the base of my Eastern redbud thrill me in spring, but there's only so much mileage I can get out of that view in late summer. I can either move the bench, or when I find another end-of-driveway cast-off, install it in another location for a new view.
- Don't underestimate the beauty of a vegetable garden when arranging seating areas. Furthermore, don't underestimate how much you'll want to sit down after harvesting your tomatoes in August. Pure exhaustion shouldn't be the only

Lead your guests to places to sit in your garden.

motivation to sit and relax, but it sure is a good one.

- If you have terrible problems with gnats or other flying insects, make sure to keep a netted hat close by. Nothing takes the fun out of sitting and observing like a gnat in the eye.

- Make sure you've got somewhere outside to enjoy an al fresco meal. Taking dinner outside gives you things to talk about, a connection to nature, and a realization of the many reasons you're working so hard during the day. Whether it's sitting on

Food from the garden is best enjoyed surrounded by that garden.

a porch step, at a patio table, or—one of my favorite memories—climbing out of a window to eat lunch on a secret roof terrace, using your outside space can make an everyday meal an event.

- Consider putting two seats together for casual conversations in different areas of your garden. When a friend visits, don't just sit on the front step, lead them to these seats with drink in hand and create a memorable moment in time.

A place to reflect

- Challenge yourself to find a single point of accomplishment in your garden every day. Something that, were you six years old again, you'd drag a parent by the hand to show off. Stare at it. Hard. Let yourself smile at the achievement.

- Consider naming areas or rooms of your garden to evoke a certain feeling or remind you of someone special. At my last house I had the Rosemary Garden, named after my mother, who spent much of her vacation helping to install it. At my new house I have christened a fern-covered embankment Fern Hill, which reminds me of one of my favorite poets, Dylan Thomas.

- If you find yourself too distracted by the garden chores around you to do much reflecting, you

I'm always so proud of my baby potatoes. Just when the plants are looking their worst, I can reach down in the soil and bring up golden treasure.

Living in the Eden You Have Created

This small garden is named after a friend whose entire life has been devoted to farming and the beauty of the garden. It's filled with a mixture of herbs, colorful perennials, and succulents.

Fighting with sweet autumn clematis every year along my porch was always worth the incredible scent that greeted us in late August. In October the plants were cut back to prevent rampant seeding.

need a prompt. Rita Perea, founder of the International Contemplative Garden Association based in Des Moines, Iowa, encourages her clients to create their own small sacred space within their garden where they can set aside the ego and "sit and be with what is." Don't kid yourself, this is a difficult exercise. But with time, it becomes easier and fosters a sense of gratitude and abundance.

- Scent is possibly the most evocative of the senses. Build fragrance into your garden and you'll find it hard to ignore the siren call drawing you away from work and toward a reflective state of mind.

A moment to connect

- Don't make the mistake of setting up a children's garden or play area without also setting up a seat for you to observe the fun and laughter. Children love to be observed, and it's a chance for you to connect with them through the garden.

- Connections with your significant other are also somehow made more magical in a garden. I rarely need to be asked to guide my husband on a personal tour of ours. Gardens (whether ours or someone else's) have always been a part of our marriage, and though it amuses and sometimes annoys me that he is oblivious to the actual daily work involved in creating and maintaining our own, I am tremendously thankful that he does appreciate the result in all its unfolding beauty, and further enjoys a few quiet moments together walking through our little kingdom—no matter how little it has been.

It doesn't need to be perfect—just comfortable. These two chairs overlook a small creek where children love to splash and catch crayfish.

- Dawn, a strong cup of black coffee, and my garden is all I need in the mornings to ground me and provide a platform for a good day. I was a stay-at-home parent and homeschooler for many years, and in the early days of small children and huge to-do lists, this was my

It's going to be a good day.

very favorite time of the day. The children were asleep, and so were many of my friends, so it felt like gifted time . . . time I didn't need to feel guilty over spending in a more productive manner. It grounded me and provided me with valuable reflection in an otherwise crazy-busy life. I'd pull an odd weed or two (depending on the severity of the infraction), but for the most part it was just a time to enjoy. It still is.

Those who work outside the home may also find that the early morning is the best time to walk and reflect in their gardens. Though dusk is a beautiful option, there are often more demands on our time and interruptions. Taking time while much of the world is still asleep but the dawn is breaking is a great habit to introduce to your day.

Living in the Eden You Have Created

An opportunity to share

- Garden parties needn't be huge soirees with orchestras, waitstaff, and a caterer. A garden party is bringing friends together in the beauty of your outside environment, whether that environment is a container-filled balcony, a small front lot, or a deck with views of surrounding rooftops. It's about celebrating your friends and family . . . and your garden. Light a few candles, invite people to bring potluck, and keep it casual. You'll stress less and entertain more.

- If you're proud of what you've created from a difficult space, don't be afraid to share it with others who might be inspired by what you have done. Getting involved with local garden clubs and tours is a great way to talk about new ideas, show off plants, and enjoy your garden in a completely new way: through the eyes of others.

- If you have flying insects that make life miserable in the garden during certain times of the year, keep a stock of netted hats and repellent in the coat closet to hand to your visitors. Don't even ask, just hand them over. This way guests don't feel like they wimped out, and you will both enjoy your time outside.

Garden parties can be as formal or informal as you wish. Consider adding a bit of sophistication to your refreshment table by filling a glass container with ice, herbs, and fruit or vegetables from the garden, and topping it with water.

Even an occasion to be critical

- We cannot pretend that as gardeners we don't get a huge amount of enjoyment from assessing our gardens and thinking about what we'd like to change or create. It's an exercise for the mind while the body is resting. If you spend that time beating yourself up, you're on the wrong track. But if you're getting so excited you have to force yourself not to stand up and get started, you've nailed it.

Big Dreams, Small Garden

Even in winter there is beauty to be observed in the garden.

- Oddly enough, the best place I know to quietly scan my garden and its progress is not actually in my garden at all. It's in my car, looking at my garden in the dead of winter as the wind blows outside and I revel in the slowly dissipating warmth. I can clearly see structures in the garden—what's wrong, what's right—and make mental notes for the spring. All without clenching my teeth against the cold. Bliss.

It's long been said, and countless times repeated, but everything is better outside. We flock to parks, to community gardens, to rivers and streams, to mountain trails and open fields to reconnect with nature even if just for a few hours.

Except now, through your own efforts, and against the odds, you've created a personal space that you can visit just by opening your door, and it's only getting better with time. Don't cheat yourself out of enjoying it.

Living in the Eden You Have Created

A PLANTSWOMAN'S GARDEN

A lot of assumptions are made when you're part of a successful family nursery and retail farm. First, that your own garden at home is extraordinary, and, second, the idea that plants are free. "Plants are never free," says Louisa Zimmermann Roberts. "And even if they were, there's no time to plant them on a seven-day-a-week schedule."

Yet her seventeen-year-old garden, located on a small lot in a small city, serves to reinforce those assumptions, boasting one of the most colorful and complex gardens it has been my privilege to visit. Does this mean late-night weeding sessions and the patience to wait for what she wants?

"Pretty much," says Louisa.

She and her husband Brian have had their ups and downs with the property—and with a challenging neighborhood—but after investing a great deal of money and energy on renovating the one hundred and twenty-year-old house only to see values slump in the area, moving has never been an option. Furthermore, Brian's exciting farm-based brewery, Mad Science Brewing Company, founded in 2013, takes all extra resources, including time.

At this point, any visitor to the wildly exuberant home and garden would have a hard time understanding why they'd want to move anyway. The front garden boasts such a varied mix of annuals, perennials, and tropicals that once past the gate, the visitor inhabits another world.

Pathways lead you past uncommon beauties and common favorites sharing bed space with a bright blue Buddha and five-foot-tall bottle trees. Fairy lights looped casually over deck railings deftly take the look into the realm of magical, and the deck s often the venue for beautiful tablescapes and late-night conversations.

"I could create the most amazing garden, but it would be nothing without sharing it with my friends," says Louisa. "A garden is a vital, living thing, and it needs human energy to thrive. It's meant for making memories. It's meant for entertainment. It's meant for sharing because there should be some reward for all the toil."

Luckily for Louisa, someone else is toiling over the food for those parties. Brian is an excellent cook, and garden space has been apportioned for his smoker and grill. But, he knows he'll always share that space with grasses and sedums and anything else Louisa's creative mind dreams up. She is always innovating, always finding new ways to showcase color and texture on a small scale.

The newest addition is a deck platform, built by Brian, that brings guests to eye level with the garden, immersing them in a comfortable living space seamlessly connected with the house and original deck. Previously, a new she shed and patio were erected at the bottom of the garden, decorated with a bohemian eye, and financed completely with the proceeds of auction items that Louisa sells at what I can only presume must be eleven o'clock at night.

It's an extraordinary garden for an extraordinarily hardworking family that serves as a getaway for many, always offering surprises to the plant-minded and non-plant-minded alike.

13

REACHING OUT AND GETTING BETTER

"A constant element of enjoyment must be mingled with our studies,
so that we think of learning as a game rather than a form of drudgery . . ."
—Desiderius Erasmus

If you love to cook, making dinner every night is guaranteed to beat that love right out of you, unless of course you are experimenting with new recipes, reading about innovative techniques, and finally figuring out how to make a perfect pâte à choux with a toddler under one arm.

If you love to garden, doing the same things out there each day, every day, is guaranteed to have a similar effect. It's why we look for new varieties of tomatoes each season or try to zone push with exotic perennials. We're trying to get better.

This is where our gardening communities come in. From the trusted words of national societies to the thrust and parry of gardening chat boards, the modern gardener is incredibly blessed with a huge amount of accessible information that can take their gardens and their gardening to a new level.

But how to get started? If you're like me, you might potter around for several years, knowing that these clubs, lectures, tours, chat groups, and websites exist, but not taking advantage of them. When you do get involved, you'll wonder why you waited.

Don't wait.

Get involved.

Here's how.

Getting involved can be as easy as helping out at a community garden and learning a few new skills from others as excited as you are.

Joining Organizations

Sitting around a dinner table on the last day of a national Garden Writers Association symposium several years ago, one of my fellow attendees, author and lecturer Mary-Kate Mackey, let out a long sigh and said, "As much as I'm looking forward to getting home, every year I feel this sadness because I'm leaving *my people*. You guys understand me; you love to talk plants!" We all laughed. We totally understood.

As much as it pains me to admit it, not everyone is a gardener. In fact, as you delve more deeply into gardening, you'll realize how few people will join you out there. That's why we need organizations and one-on-one relationships with others who share our passion, which can prevent us from drowning our "normal" friends and family in plant-themed conversations all the time. Here are four ways to consider getting involved, ranked in order of their time and/or money commitment.

When you join organizations, you give yourself an opportunity to meet and travel with people who are just as obsessed with plants as you are.

Social media

If you're already on social media, why not use it to build your circle of gardening contacts? Though I wouldn't encourage this as your only contact with other gardeners, being able to ask (and answer) questions of knowledgeable and enthusiastic members while in your pajamas is pretty terrific.

It's also a great way to start broadening your knowledge in specific areas. From growing tropical plants in distinctly non-tropical environments, to foraging for edibles in your neighborhood, you can find a group that suits your needs.

Local clubs

Local clubs in your area can be formal or informal, but they're always hungry for new members. If they prefer to approach you after you've been suitably vetted, chances are they hearken back to a blue-blood past where membership in a garden club required a twinset and a toy dog. Don't worry, you're not missing much besides a sense of inadequacy over your china pattern.

Thankfully, there are many other options. Some are grouped around a particular interest or lifestyle, some around a geographical location, others are all about a certain plant. Show a bit of interest during a garden tour or strike up a conversation at a nursery and there's a good chance you'll be asked for your email address. Hand it over.

Remember, networking isn't necessarily about building a career, it's about creating a web of friends and experts who help each other in a specific interest or discipline. In return for a small dues payment, local clubs usually have speakers, arrange tours, give workshops,

A local garden club helps rescue plants from a home about to be sold. How will you ever find out about events like this if you don't join a club yourself?

and generally enhance your gardening life. They also offer a wealth of opportunities for getting involved, such as contacting speakers, arranging tours, giving workshops, and, well, you get the picture.

National societies

In a digital world, membership in these valuable academic organizations is sadly dwindling. Yet they provide some of the best monthly or quarterly journals, speakers, symposiums, and opportunities for fine-tuning the gardener's knowledge base.

Start with the American Horticultural Society, and then explore your plant passions with membership in a more specific society, such as the Pacific Bulb Society or the North American Rock Garden Society. These dues-based organizations are not expensive, and they'll welcome you with open arms—and encourage you to join your local chapter so you can connect with people just down the street who go nuts over the same stuff you do.

Master Gardener program

You don't have to be a master gardener to want to become a Master Gardener. All you need is enthusiasm, a desire to study, and a willingness to give back to your community. The Master Gardener program is present in all fifty states and Canada, and with the exception of Massachusetts and the Canadian provinces, administered through a state's land-grant university or cooperative extension service.

The aim of the Master Gardener program is to provide trained volunteers within communities to promote agricultural endeavors and distribute horticultural information to the public, usually on a county level. Depending on the state requirements, interns complete forty to sixty hours of classroom instruction, covering everything from basic botany to composting. Volunteers then assist in their communities each year, answering questions, maintaining demo gardens, giving presentations, and doing many other worthwhile activities. Whether you like to talk in front of people or remain in the background, there is a place for you in Master Gardeners.

There is a fee to cover course materials, but financial aid programs do exist to help with the cost. In addition, some counties have night classes, so people who work during the day or stay home with children (that was me!) have the opportunity to join a group of enthusiastic gardeners over eighty thousand strong[1].

Plants wait for buyers at an annual Master Gardener plant sale—a fun and productive event for many local gardeners in counties all over the United States.

Tours

Where self-study is concerned, going on a garden tour almost feels like cheating. You get to look at marvelous plants, consider exquisite designs, and talk with people as interested in plants as you are.

Many cities and towns have garden tours during the high season of May and June, but joining an organization (see below) will allow you to be part of free tours that aren't advertised to the general public. Go. See other gardens. There you will find new ideas and ways of dealing with difficult spaces that thrill you so much you'll go home and dig holes for six hours.

Tours can be formal or informal, but they'll always give you ideas.

You're going to see some pretty special gardens, and, no doubt, some very expensive gardens. Don't spend your time wondering how much money it took to create those rock

---

1 2014 Extension Master Gardener Survey.

walls or that beech hedge. Instead, take your camera, take a notebook, and modify the designs of others to suit your space and your budget.

Lectures

If you weren't very academic in school, the thought of attending a lecture may trigger an immediate desire to fall asleep. It's okay. You're an adult now. You *want* to learn more about plants, and no one is going to quiz you at the end.

And, in order to gain admittance, you don't have to: a) be eighty-five; b) know how to crochet; or c) speak Latin. It's not that kind of horticultural world anymore. Thanks to a back-to-the-earth resurgence and a new understanding of the importance of fresh, locally grown foods, gardening is hip again. Consequently, the vast majority of speakers out there are ready to connect young, hashtagging dirt hounds to new concepts, new methods, and new people.

Books and blogs are great, but listening to a kindred spirit speak about a topic that fascinates you, and having the subsequent ability to discuss that topic, takes education to another level. Getting in the habit of doing this sooner rather than later in your career or hobby will open doors to opportunities and friendships that you might not otherwise know existed.

Let's consider the types of speakers out there:

1. **Speaker presents on behalf of local groups**—Local clubs and organizations are the cheapest and easiest way to dip your feet into the lecture world, and the talks are usually free. Give up a weeknight, take away new information and a new contact or two.

2. **Speaker is a plant-world rock star**—If you're lucky enough to belong to or live near a club that's willing to pay for well-known speakers, you'd be insane not to give up an evening. It's a small investment to pay ten dollars to hear Alexis Datta, the former head gardener at Sissinghurst Castle Garden, tell you a thing or two about borders, or Panayoti Kelaidis, senior curator of plant collections at Denver Botanic Gardens, tell you how he got into gardening in the first place.

3. **Speaker is ultimately selling a book or product**—Buying Amy Stewart's *The Drunken Botanist* could be perceived as a direct result of the gin and tonic reception before her lecture, but it was actually her witty presentation and fascinating topic that had me handing over the plastic card. Hearing an author speak profoundly enhances your connection with the words they have written.

Don't forget to bring a notebook and *mingle*. You might not have the opportunity to talk with this lecturer again—take advantage of it!

The Digital Community

Thanks to the Internet, if you're a beginner gardener you can ask everything from "What is a seed?" to "What does soil do?" and rest easy in the knowledge that only you and the NSA are aware of your ignorance.

I only wish that, like all power tools, the Internet came with a user's manual. The tradeoff one makes in having access to a flood of information is having access to a flood of *mis*information. Here are just a few examples of the ways in which you may literally be led down the garden path.

Whether it's seeds, plants, information, or just a bit of horticultural humor, you can find what you need on the web.

1. **The copied misinformation:** There are a lot of bloggers out there writing for free or thereabouts and regurgitating information without testing any of it. That's precisely why you salted your soil to kill weeds last week and now have about as much chance of growing anything there as the Carthaginians did after the Punic Wars. Copying is fine if they're using www.usda.gov and citing their sources, but not so great if they're just Googling in the darkness like you.

2. **The oft-repeated myths:** For instance, "Use a windowsill to start seedlings [*and you'll end up with leggy seedlings*]." or "Blast aphids off flower heads with a strong jet of water [*and destroy both the flower AND the aphids*]." Some advice is very well known and oft repeated, but put into practice it can lead to frustration.

3. **The too-good-to-be-true photos:** How many lies are told every day with a camera? Don't kid yourself that it's only happening in Los Angeles. One of my favorites is the shot of plump farmyard chickens wandering through a beautiful vegetable garden. Go ahead. Put Henny Penny in your gorgeous creation for three unsupervised hours and see what happens. I'm a huge fan of Ms. P. pecking at your plot, but about one month before you actually plant anything.

4. **The salesman vortex:** There are online nurseries out there who are not above stretching the truth a little to sell a plant. If you want good information on a specific plant, it may not be wise to get all your information from the person who is invested in selling it to you.

Basically you're navigating a minefield, and you've got to know where to put your feet safely. You're going to make mistakes, but here are some tips on getting started.

1. **Look for university or government-based sites:** Some horticultural studies take months, years, even decades to complete. Take advantage of the data all that grant money paid for and peruse the .edu and .gov sites first.

2. **Find out where the author/blogger/freelancer writes:** A Zone 10 Florida gardener may actually be able to say "start your seedlings on a sunny patio" and be right on the money . . . for other Zone 10 gardeners. Location is critical when you're applying gardening advice, so be sure to know their zone *and* your own.

3. **Check out peer-reviewed books at the library:** Though it can happen, having several knowledgeable editors on their back makes it harder for an author to put misinformation into print. (Boy, I'm just asking for it, aren't I?) This is not so on the World Wide Web. If information is inaccurate, it may be challenged by a commenter trolling the Internet, but faced with entering my name, creating a password, and deciphering the CAPTCHA, all in order to correct the blogger and tell people **not** to plant poppy seeds in the spring in the mid-Atlantic, I and many others have usually lost interest and moved on to YouTube videos of Chanticleer Garden in the spring.

4. **Cross-check, cross-check, cross-check:** This can be as simple as finding a good forum with lots of active, outspoken members, or finding several individual sites that you like and can contrast with one another. If they all say something different (and they can), either use the most conservative opinion to avoid losing money and time, or go back to respected, last-word-on-the-subject manuals, such as the *American Horticultural Society A-Z Encyclopedia of Garden Plants*.

Building a library of trusted gardening books is invaluable to the home gardener.

Don't forget to take a few moments to actually ponder and perhaps write down what you are reading and experiencing. Here's where your journal comes in.

Go on, move beyond the confines of your own garden walls. If you're not growing as a gardener, you'll soon find drudgery where before there was joy. There may be limits on your gardening space, but there are no limits on your gardening mind. Cultivate it and who knows how far you'll go.

A FORMAL TOWN GARDEN

Sonya and Lee Hand have always been attracted to the charm and solidity of historic homes. In fact, dreams of an old home and land were one of the things over which they first connected during their dating years at the University of Virginia.

Standing in the fenced back garden of their home of fourteen years, it appears that they got exactly what they longed for. A clapboard summer kitchen and smokehouse anchor the classic formal gardens, and a weathered, rusty red carriage house draws the eye back through fruit trees, vegetable beds, and gravel paths. The garden has all the charm and presence of a Georgetown courtyard, but things have changed a great deal in this Northern Maryland town since the house was built in 1890.

Perched on a very busy thoroughfare, its cheerful yellow siding is a martyr to dust and grime, and a biker bar and town siren not too far away mean things can get noisy on the weekend. Sonya and Lee have had their ups and downs with a string of neighbors in the rental house next door, dealing with everything from domestic arguments to cigarette butts thrown over the fence. It's not the idealized country home they dreamed of, yet the

...ouse called to them for several reasons, not
...east of all their small budget.

"It was a family home," says Sonya. "You
...ould feel that when you walked in."

They ran with that feeling as they created a
...garden around their own three busy children.
...he summer house was used as a playroom,
...hen a schoolroom, and now an office for
...onya, who is the director of business training
...and services for a local community college.

Winding paths lead happy feet past a
...bubbling fountain in an antique claw-foot tub
...o a wooden playset and seating area behind
...he old carriage house. Herbs and salad
...vegetables in brick beds surround a seating
...area where children celebrate birthdays and

friends gather for barbecues. From stones to bricks
to timber to that antique tub, the majority of the
hardscaping materials have been reclaimed through
free sources.

"I always wanted enough space for horses and
a pool," says Sonya, "but in many ways, this garden
fits us much better. It's just enough for us to handle
and still have balance in our work and home lives."

Lee, who is the assistant principal of a classical
charter school, agrees. He's spent many happy hours in
this garden, but is realistic about the amount of work
it takes to create and maintain it. "Is it worth it?" I ask
him—knowing he's been fighting Bermuda grass from
the neighbor's property in preparation for my visit.

"Absolutely," he says with a cheerful grin. "At the
end of the day, when we're all outside, and the sun's
going down, it's a pretty cool place to be."

14

CULTIVATING A SPIRIT OF CONTENTMENT

"Be happy for this moment. This moment is your life."
—Omar Khayyám

Just because one day you begin to garden, doesn't mean your feelings of envy, resentment, bitterness, or anger will miraculously disappear the next. It's a process that is certainly facilitated by the quiet wisdom of the garden working through us, but it also takes some work on our part. And in a media-saturated world, we've got our work cut out for us.

Everywhere we look we're confronted by images of others who appear to be gardening, cooking, exercising, traveling, or just plain living, better than we are. If the copious postings of our "closest friends" on social media sites weren't enough to convince us of our total inadequacy as human beings, we can always open a magazine at the checkout counter or surf online in the evening and thoroughly wallow in how beautiful the lives, gardens, houses, parties, and vacations of others are, especially compared to the banality and simplicity of our own.

Pick up one of those lifestyle magazines. Gasp at the beauty of sedums and succulents expertly arranged into a necklace for a high-society bride. Three pages later you'll find a community garden party lit entirely by hanging tea lights in mason jars as guests sip signature cocktails and presumably discuss heirloom seed saving until the wee small hours. If present, children are small and discreet and always dressed in white linen.

Then walk outside and look at your own garden.

God knows you love it. Dedicate hours of your life to it. Credit it for healing your outlook, your attitude, and your sense of humor . . . *but is it as good as theirs?*

In a dark corner there's a four-week-old pile of browned and vicious rose canes. Over there a galvanized pail filled with oily water and wiggling mosquito larvae. Here a strawberry six-pack that never went into the ground in May. The grass is long. The pots are wilting. The roses have black spot.

But not those roses on your computer screen. Oh no. From the looks of things they've never known anything but the purest of health in the best of conditions in the kindest of lights.

No matter how centered your outlook, it's hard to not feel like you're falling behind. Maybe you've also had a bad week, or a bad month, or have stared too long at your neighbor's brand-new Mercedes and have allowed yourself to revisit old feelings of injustice.

"Comparing ourselves to others—judgment—is the last addiction to break," says Rita Perea, founder of the International Contemplative Garden Association. "You must have a process or many processes in place to recognize and deal with that."

How can we find those processes? How can we rise above the thoughts that threaten to overwhelm us sometimes? How can our gardens help?

Let go of comparisons and *observe*

Trust me when I tell you that our lives (particularly our lives in the garden) are made up of a thousand still lifes, sound bites, video clips, and slow-motion moments every day; we just don't see them. Sometimes we are lucky enough to have an artistically observant friend record an event, place, or moment for us and present us with the polished result, but generally these moments pass us by and we assume they don't exist.

I know this because I know how to use a camera, a device that can change the ordinary to the extraordinary in a fraction of a second. I'm not the world's best photographer, but where my skill ends, *I know others who know how to use a camera.*

I've stood in gardens that haven't thrilled me and seen drop-dead gorgeous photographs of the same garden on the same day at the same hour. I've seen photographers on their stomachs in mud capturing the intricacies of a single bloom when the actual garden or greenhouse that surrounded it was a chaotic mess. I've watched a garden tableau artistically and frantically arranged for a photo, and then ripped apart again as soon as the shoot was over.

Such knowledge and experience is incredibly powerful. It's the equivalent of standing before Superman with a lump of Kryptonite in my hand. I can appreciate a photo for its artistic merits, attention to detail, and ability to stir emotional response, but I also know that any other assumptions I make about it are probably false.

I don't want you to stop viewing these images or to block them out. There's far too much to be gained by studying and enjoying them. I just want you to see them for what they are: a constructed view, a forced perspective, a work of art.

Take a few minutes in the early morning to find your own still lifes. Observe the pairing of a Boston fern resting on your porch next to a soil-encrusted trowel or a bowl of pansies planted in a worn terracotta pot.

Now, *really* look at them. The salt crystals on the terracotta, the contrasts of purple and gold, the fresh goodness of the soil. On a tight off-center focus, they are magically transformed into fine art. There are still lifes in your kitchens . . . in your living rooms . . . in the freshly washed stack of towels sitting on a cluttered table waiting to be put away. Ignore the mess behind them or, better yet, make it a still life of its own.

Use your own phone or camera, fiddle around with some automatic filters. *Try it for yourself.* And even if you simply can't capture that moment on screen, at least you took a moment to observe it in the first place. Tuck that observation away and reflect upon it when you insist upon stalking the Facebook page of your greatest high school rival. Once you've figured out that there is a wizard behind that curtain, you'll spend a lot less time beating yourself up and a lot more time seeing your own magazine moments in the garden.

Let go of negativity and *engage*

Nowhere is the lifelong metaphorical journey of change and growth more physically evident than in a garden. Adaptation, struggle, perseverance, victory, loss, quiet dormancy and exquisite rebirth—all are on view to the observant gardener with heart and hands connected to the soil.

Is it any wonder then that witnessing and experiencing such events on a daily basis can have a remarkable healing effect on the individual who is feeling battered and bruised by a hectic week or a difficult period in life?

"My house and garden is an accomplishment that matters, even when the world doesn't think I can do anything it wants done," says Jerry Cayford, one of our profile gardeners who spent two years searching for work after a layoff. "Making a wonderful place to live was a great source of security and self-esteem when both were in short supply."

Watching one's garden instinctively respond to challenging circumstances and quietly adapt to them enriches the soul, providing a template for those who have forgotten the benefits of letting go and adapting their lives to equally challenging conditions. Further

engaging with those processes and actually having a hand in the creation of something beautiful—something functional and useful—is a huge step in reclaiming one's sense of joy.

What might have been the alternative? Holding on to anger? Allowing your sense of injustice and feelings of resentment to keep you paralyzed? We are only given one life on this earth. Stagnation should not be an option for someone with a gardener's heart.

Even for someone with a bog-gardener's heart.

Let go of stress and *absorb*

"I've enjoyed the tranquility of gardens since I was a child," says Anita Avent, founder of the Center for Mindfulness and Nonduality at Juniper Level Botanic Garden in Raleigh, North Carolina, and wife of well-known plant explorer Tony Avent. "[I] have come to see the gardens as a wise teacher, always pointing us toward the ineffable omnipresence that simply is . . . teaching us to surrender, yield, and be fluid," she adds.

Juniper Level Botanic Garden is also home to the plant collector's paradise, Plant Delights. Running one of the most successful mail order nurseries and plant research facilities on the East Coast can be incredibly stressful, but, thankfully, there is always the garden in which to unwind.

"Tony and I walk the gardens meditatively at the end of most workdays. We shed the hectic energy of managing the nursery, feeling it draining out through our feet back into the earth," she writes in her blog.[2]

That is the gift of the garden. It gives us a place to shed negative energy, either through the demands of hard physical work or through quiet meditation.

Quiet your mind and it will fill each and every one of your senses. You'll catch the bright scent of sunlight on vegetation and feel the texture of a soft lamb's ear or prickly aloe. You'll taste the tender sweetness of a just-picked strawberry. You'll hear a soft rustle and lose yourself for several minutes watching the cats play hide-and-go-seek amongst tufts of dried grass.

And when you are feeling world-weary, what a lift you can experience knowing that you are responsible for this beautiful space, this sanctuary, where before there was nothing.

Let go of cynicism and *choose*

Unlike our plants, which instinctively adjust toward a state of well-being, living in a state of contentment is a decision that we, as human beings, must make every day. Some of us do this unconsciously, and some of us must train ourselves to see the joy in conquering adversity, knowing that it takes time to build a habit of mind.

I will admit that I belong to the latter group. When a car cuts me off on the freeway, I don't assume the driver is racing to the hospital, I assume the driver is a narcissistic idiot. When my children leave their backpacks, coats, shoes, and moldy lunch bags on the dining room table yet again, I don't assume that they're just being careless. I assume that they are deliberately trying to provoke a nervous breakdown just to see what it looks like.

---

2 Anita Avent, "Touching the Sole," www.mindfulnessandnonduality.org.

No matter how much yoga I practice and healthy foods I eat, I continually have to choose to be happy, choose to see the good, choose to ignore or laugh at the bad.

Except, that is, when I am in the garden. Suddenly that choice is instinctive—I don't think about it for a second.

- When I see a tiny self-seeded cyclamen in the lawn I am elated. No matter that I've been killing myself to encourage a colony somewhere else and this little plant is slapping me in the face with its vitality.
- When I lose a beloved plant to a wicked cold snap, I am over it within a few minutes, already planning for a new arrival.
- When my hands are frozen after wrestling with a chicken waterer for fifteen minutes, the antics of my backyard flock mesmerize me for a half an hour and it calms the annoyance right out of me.

The garden teaches me that I—a master cynic and lifelong professor of sarcasm—have the potential to greet every situation in a positive way. When I don't, it gives me the opportunity to come back, center myself in a quiet, enriching environment, and try again.

Let go of anxiety and *be mindful*

According to Rita Perea, mindfulness is "being fully present in the moment." A leadership consultant, Rita has worked with many clients over the years, but she saw a disturbing trend after the economic events of 2008.

"I met many people who were at a breaking point after losing their jobs, and many more who were burned out at jobs they were terrified to lose, but which expected so much more from them," she recalls.

She found that bringing clients into the quiet and sanctity of her city garden helped them enormously, allowing them to reconnect with the present moment and with their place in the natural world. Observing the beauty in something as small as a rounded stone or hearing the sound of water falling in a nearby fountain . . . these simple, timeless truths could only be observed by a quiet mind.

Is mindfulness a new concept for a new generation? If you asked my father, he might stumble over the terminology, but once apprised of it, he'd answer no. After all, he's been practicing a form of mindfulness most of his adult life, living with purpose and deliberation, aware of each moment, and letting the quiet routine of his outside life bring calm and peacefulness to his work life indoors.

And he certainly wasn't the first.

It's easy to make excuses for our lack of mindfulness these days. We have phones, email, social media, schedules that make our grandparents' eyes water, and very little time for contemplative practices. We're accomplishing much, yet we're cheating ourselves out of enjoying any of it.

Enter our garden. Time spent there (especially if we've left our devices safely charging inside) is time to effortlessly apply mindful principles in all that we do, letting the earth-centered nature of our tasks ground us to each moment.

Those are moments without anxiety and stress. Those are moments of contentment . . . of mindfulness. My father would just call it "paying attention."

Paradoxically, technology can sometimes aid busy minds to find these moments. A friend of mine who passed away six years ago regularly used her phone to help her connect to a specific minute each night, although it all started quite comically.

After fiddling with the alarm on a new pager, her husband could not get it to stop ringing every night at 8:13 p.m. This went on for a week, until, inspired by the continuity of being alerted to absolutely nothing at all at precisely the same time every evening, Jeanne set her own alarm and began to journal what they were both doing when it went off. Whether it was in the garden or out with friends, feeding dogs or still at work, she took the time to observe and express what was happening—good or bad.

I am a terrible journaler, but the wisdom of this practice inspired me to set a similar alarm. And in the summertime, especially during the week, it usually finds me in the garden frantically finishing up a task before the light fades. For someone like myself—ever busy, ever productive—this alarm stops me for a moment and gently prompts me to absorb that moment for its sights, smells, sounds, textures, and sometimes even tastes. So I keep my phone with me, but only allow alarm notification in the evenings to prevent other techno-distractions that would negate the practice.

Cultivating a Spirit of Contentment

My absolute favorite 8:13 moment is one spent in the company of friends sharing dinner or drinks in the garden. It is a simple legacy from a friend, but a profound one nonetheless.

Observe, engage, absorb, choose, or be mindful—or you can just plunge your hands in the dirt and let it happen

Gardeners have always felt it to be true, but studies conducted over the last two decades have found that there might be a bit of science behind the old adage that digging in the dirt makes you happier.

It all has to do with a naturally occurring bacteria in the soil, *Mycobacterium vaccae*. *M. vaccae* appears to have a significant effect on serotonin levels in the brains of mice, positively affecting anti-anxiety behaviors when ingested or inhaled.[3] Injectable *M. vaccae* has also been used in studies to treat small cell lung cancer patients during chemotherapy, with patients relating a greater sense of well-being, less pain and nausea during treatment, and a trend toward improved median survival.[4]

A study in 2013 showed that mice fed strains of *M. vaccae* made it through mazes in half the time of the control group, with less anxiety behaviors.[5] These studies all suggest that after millions of years of evolution, animal immune systems may be symbiotically enhanced by ambient microbes, giving them some level of protection from pathogens—or maybe just from having a bad day.

In short: soil makes us happy.

So breathe a little deeper out there. Don't be afraid to ingest a bit of dirt when you pick a warm strawberry or a baby carrot out of the fresh soil and just can't wait to get back to the sink. That connection to the earth is millions of years old, and an instinctual knowledge of it is probably what made you pick up a trowel in the first place.

Don't overthink it

Each year, when the softly pointed shoots of lily of the valley break through the spring soil, I am reminded of our capacity to rebound as human beings. This humble little plant well

---

3 Lowry, et al, 2007.

4 Assersohn, et al, 2002.

5 Matthews, Jenks, 2013.

deserves its place in floriography as a symbol of a return to happiness. Year after year it grows, buds, flowers, and dies back, returning stronger every spring, even in the face of my brutal mid-Atlantic winters. A single sprig of blossom will fill my entire kitchen with scent, hitting me over the head with the profound truth that life is good boiled down to the simplest of pleasures.

Contentment is such a simple concept. We complicate it with what we think we need, what we think we should be, what we perceive others to be. None of this matters in our garden.

We are not consumers there. We are stewards. We care for and are enriched by that small bit of soil, that potted terrace, that vegetable bed connecting us back to our roots as gatherers and as gardeners.

Whatever space you've been given, use it to guide you back to that place. Use it to create your own Eden on earth.

PROFILE: CAROLE GALATI

NO-MOW PARADISE

" **E**veryone is an inspiration to someone else," Carole Galati tells me over the phone the week before I visit her garden in a crowded older suburb of Washington, D.C. "Everyone starts somewhere."

But when I learn where she started, as a single mother working as a teacher with the heavy burden of student loans to manage, I am even more inspired by the mature garden that surrounds the modest Cape Cod home and practically tumbles over itself to greet me. A garden that showcases an exuberance that is delightfully at odds with the tidy, unremarkable lawn and foundation plantings of her neighbors.

It is even more inspiring when she tells me what the suburban asphalt hides.

"A tributary of Sligo Creek was paved over to create the subdivision," explains Carole with a wry smile. Except it seems no one told the tributary.

Carole has been dealing with severe water issues all forty-five of her years at the property.

Laughing, she says, "There were times that the torrent of water coming down the street and into the garden was so strong that I was chasing uprooted plants down the street!" Four decades later, the seasonal torrent remains, but it's Carole's creative response to the challenge that allowed her to plant a front garden that was featured in *The Washington Post* several years ago as a stunning example of homes that have "Lost the Lawn."

Always conscious of the bottom line ("Almost like a Depression baby," says Carole), she used reclaimed railroad ties and stone to create a barrier to divert the water back onto the paved surfaces of sidewalk and road. Her heavy clay soil has become fertile and sponge-like after years of adding leaf mulch by the bucketful from the local municipality.

There is no grass here, but in its place there are redbuds, hydrangea, dogwoods, and a host of native plants that can handle a bit of moisture. Where drier conditions are desired, Carole has built up some beds, creating a topography that is not only sensible, but visually appealing.

Carole is a member of five different garden clubs and credits the knowledge and friendships she has made for the remarkable diversity of plants that inhabit her garden. Her advice to gardeners looking at difficult spaces? "Chunk it off," advises this quiet, lovely woman surrounded by a lifetime's project. "Don't do too much at once."

Looking around at the many layers that make up this spectacular garden, it's hard to be sure that she ever took her own advice.

EPILOGUE

"I've finally finished!"
—said no gardener ever

Although the creation of a beautiful garden in an imperfect space was certainly a happy ending to our story, there is yet another chapter to this tale. After years of actively looking for more land at a price we could afford, we were fortunate to find a beautiful home and property a mere three miles from our home of over ten years. And, due to the careful use of resources over the previous twenty, we were able to afford it.

In our new home we can explore many of our long-held desires, such as having legal chickens and more than two beehives. We can heat our house with wood from the property and tramp through those woods to find new species of edible mushrooms. (Or, at least I can. My husband is convinced I'm trying to poison him.)

After a day spent battling aggressive vines and Japanese stiltgrass, stacking wood, or creating a brand-new bed where none existed, I often smile at the old adage, "be careful what you wish for," and I think back on the manageability and charm of my previous smaller gardens, and a back that was twenty years younger.

But I wouldn't change anything. I know those other gardens were a primer for this one—necessary in my education as a gardener, a writer, and a human being. For how can we truly appreciate something without knowing its absence? My last garden gave me purpose, joy, and a steady connection to the outside world when I wanted to feel sorry for myself and angry over events I couldn't control.

We never abandoned our dreams, we just chose to be happy while searching for them. The point is the journey. What better than a garden to teach us that?

I wish you luck on your own journey. It will be different than mine. It will be different than the journey of the heiress and her garden designer. But what it will no doubt share with all of us is a deep connection with the earth and with each other as gardeners, whether rich, poor, or somewhere in between.

—Marianne

WORKS CITED

1 2014 Extension Master Gardener Survey, Extension Master Gardener National Committee (EMGNC).

2 Avent, Anita. "Touching the Sole." Web blog post. Center for Mindfulness and Nonduality at Juniper Level Botanic Garden. www.mindfulnessandnonduality.org. August 29, 2015.

3 Lowry, et al. "Identification of an immune-responsive mesolimbocortical serotonergic system: potential role in regulation of emotional behavior." *Neuroscience.* 146(2) (May 2007) 756–772.

4 Assersohn, et al. "A randomized pilot study of SRL172 (*Mycobacterium vaccae*) in patients with small cell lung cancer (SCLC) treated with chemotherapy." *Clinical Oncology.* 14(1) (February 2002) 23–27.

5 Matthews, Dorothy M., Jenks, Susan M. "Ingestion of *Mycobacterium vaccae* decreases anxiety-related behavior and improves learning in mice." *Behavioural Processes.* 96 (June 2013) 27–35.

RECOMMENDED BOOKS

Bartholomew, Mel. *All New Square Foot Gardening*. Minneapolis: Cool Springs Press, 2013.

Brickell, Christopher and Joyce, David. *American Horticultural Society Pruning and Training*. London: Dorling Kindersley, 2011.

Coleman, Eliot. *Four-Season Harvest: Organic Vegetables from Your Home Garden All Year Long*. White River Junction: Chelsea Green Publishing, 1999.

Dacyczyn, Amy. *The Complete Tightwad Gazette: Promoting Thrift as a Viable Alternative Lifestyle*. New York: Villard Books, 1998.

Hill, Lewis. *Secrets of Plant Propagation*. North Adams: Storey Publishing, 1985.

Lloyd, Christopher and Rice, Graham. *Garden Flowers from Seed*. Portland: Timber Press, 1991.

Lowe, Judy. *Ortho's All About Pruning*. Des Moines: Meredith Books, 1999.

Silber, Terry and Mark. *Growing Herbs and Vegetables: From seed to harvest*. New York: Alfred A. Knopf, 1999.

ACKNOWLEDGMENTS

My grateful thanks to those who opened their gardens and their hearts to me during the course of writing this book, to those that provided photographs, and to the expects and designers who took time from busy schedules to help me in my quest to energize and encourage the tentative gardener that lives within so many of us.

And to my editor, Brooke Rockwell, who with patient words and a sense of humor, guided me through the process of sharing that vision with readers.

Photo Credits (in order of appearance)

All photos taken by the author (©MB Willburn), unless noted below:

©Rosemary Bowly, p. 4, 23 (top right), 123, 147
©Daniel Weil, p. 6, 29 (top right), 90 (bottom left), 91, 118 (bottom left), 132 (top right), 133 (bottom right), 171 (top right), 192–193
©John Boggan, p. 11
©Urban Homestead, p. 14–15
©Susan Harris, p. 31
©Louise Handley, p. 40–41
©Kat Forder, p. 67
©Ken Burris, p. 65
©Sheila Cassani, p. 102–103
©Sheryl Massaro, p. 145 (top left)
©Steven Biggs, p. 158–159
©Kelly Fowler, p. 162
©Sonya Hand, p. 181 (bottom left)

Photo Location Acknowledgements (in order of appearance)

(in consideration of privacy, private gardens are listed without location)

Walnut Hill, The Garden of A.C. & Penney Hubbard, p. x, 32 (left)
The Kendall Garden, p. xiii
The Huntington Library, Art Collections and Botanical Gardens, San Marino, CA, p. 18, 187

The Portland Japanese Garden, Portland, OR, p. 19 (top)
West Dean Gardens, West Dean, Sussex, UK, p. 19 (bottom)
The Garden of Jerry Cayford & Karin Birch, p. 28–29, 164,
High Glen Gardens, p. 36
The Garden of Mary Price, p. 45 (right center)
Reverie, Pittsburgh, PA, p. 45 (bottom right)
Longwood Gardens, Kennett Square, PA, p. 49
The Garden of Amy & Chris Hebert, p. 56–57
The Garden of Louisa & Brian Roberts, p. 60, 66 (top right), 97, 170–171
Chanticleer Garden, Wayne, PA, p. 66 (center), 72 (top)
Lewis Ginter Botanical Garden, Henrico, VA, p. 69 (bottom)
Bird Hill, Free Union, VA, p. 71 (center), 87
Los Angeles County Arboretum and Botanic Garden, 72 (bottom), 79
The Garden of Clifford & Judith Coote, p. 73
Thanksgiving Farms, Frederick, MD, p. 74
The Garden of Lee Dunn, p. 76
The Garden of Jan Faulkner, p. 90–91
The Frederick News Post Community Garden, Frederick, MD, p. 93, 132–133
The Garden of Jennifer & Eric Knowles, p. 96, 148–149
The Garden of Paul Lehmann & Jeannie Goforth, p. 118–119
The Garden of Sonya & Lee Hand, p. 141 (bottom), 180–181, 184
The Garden of Sheryl Massaro, p. 144–145
The Garden of Bill and Linda Pinkham, p. 146
The Garden of Ellis Burruss & Jane Weisemann, p. 150
The Brunswick Community Garden, Brunswick, MD, p. 151, 157, 173
The Sierra Waldorf School, Jamestown, CA, p. 152–153
Four Winds Cellars, Vallecito, CA, p. 168
The Garden of Ron & Norma Brown, p. 172
The Garden of James Dronenburg & Daniel Weil, p. 186
The Garden of Bob & Bobbie Diebold, p. 191
The Garden of Carole Galati, p. 192–193

Big Dreams, Small Garden

Obstacles & Opportunities Worksheet

These obstacles:

⬇

Could become these opportunities:

⬇

Big Dreams, Small Garden

Project Worksheet

Goal:	
Budget:	$
Priority:	☐ Low ☐ Medium ☐ High
Timing:	
Materials needed:	
Possible resources:	
Notes:	

Date Completed: _____

Actual Cost: $ _____

Big Dreams, Small Garden

Garden Notes

Plant Name	Location	Date Planted	Notes

Big Dreams, Small Garden

Garden Notes

Plant Name	Location	Date Planted	Notes